GARTH BROOKS

• THE LIMITED SERIES •

D1302949

Editor's Note: A very special thank you to Lana Thrasher for her loyalty and contribution to the production of this songbook. It is my personal pleasure to work with such an exceptional lady.

Project Manager / Editor: Carol Cuellar
Book Layout: WordWorks, Inc.

Management: Bob Doyle and Kelly Brooks, GB Management, Nashville, TN
Fan Club: The Believer Magazine, PO Box 507, Goodlettsville, TN 37070. (615) 859.5336
e-mail: garthbrooks@earthlink.net / Merchandise website: www.garthstore.com
Also available: *Garth Live From Central Park* (video) 10119 / *Sevens* (CD and cassette) 56599
Photography: Beverly Parker

Garth Brooks jump-started country music at the beginning of the decade, raising its worldwide visibility and prestige to an unprecedented level and going on to become the biggest selling solo artist in U.S. music history with more than 62 million albums sold. He is also the fastest selling album artist in RIAA history and one of the industry's most awarded, with the latest nod coming from the Country Music Association when the organization named him its 1997 Entertainer of the Year.

Last year he infused new energy into country when he played to the largest crowd ever to attend a concert in New York's Central Park, a performance viewed by an additional TV audience of 14.6 million people. His 1997 tour attracted more than 3 million fans since Garth hit the road last March. What those statistics mean is that tremendous numbers of people are touched by what Garth Brooks loves to do...........make music.

Album statistics: His debut Album, *Garth Brooks*, released in 1989, was the biggest selling country album of the 1980s. His sophomore outing, *No Fences*, is the biggest selling country album of all time. *Ropin' The Wind* was the third biggest and the first album to debut at #1 on both the Billboard Top 200 Album chart and the Billboard Country Album Chart. *The Chase* and *In Pieces* both entered the pop and country charts at #1.

Garth has made four NBC specials, all of which were overwhelming ratings successes. The first special, *This Is Garth Brooks*, was filmed at Dallas' Reunion Arena in September 1991. At the time it aired, it gave NBC its highest rated Friday night in more than two years (17.3 rating/28 share), and was the #9 show in the Nielsen ratings for the week. The second airing of *This Is Garth Brooks* remained powerful, receiving a 6.9 rating and a 12 share. *This Is Garth Brooks, Too!* was filmed over the course of three sold-out shows at Texas Stadium in Dallas in 1993, and that show gave NBC its first time period win among adults (18–49) since August 1992.

When *The Hits* aired in January of 1995, it gave NBC its best adult rating in that time slot since January 19, 1994, with an 11.8 rating and an 18 share. The behind-the-scenes documentary, *Trying To Rope The World*, featured never-before-seen footage of Garth's first European/Australian tour in 1994 and received a 9.4 rating and a 15 share in the 18–49 demographics.

In December of 1996, VH1 premiered *Garth Brooks: Storytellers*, as part of its critically acclaimed singer/songwriter series. This intimate look into Garth and his music doubled the ratings of shows featuring rock stars including Sting, Jackson Browne, Elvis Costello and Melissa Etheridge.

Garth — Live From Central Park first aired August 7, 1997. The spectacular was the most watched and highest rated original program on HBO in 1997, beating all broadcast competition in the time period, as well as three of the four networks combined. New York ratings were an amazing 51.7 according to Nielsen. The 1997 Super Bowl did not do as well. Ratings continued to rise throughout the evening of the concert, peaking at a 19.1/29 in the last 15 minutes of the concert. Based on HBO average ratings, *Garth — Live From Central Park* was the most watched special on cable television in 1997.

Along with the sales came awards, including a Grammy, 11 American Music Awards, 10 Country Music Association Awards, 14 Academy of Country Music Awards, 5 World Music Awards and 8 People's Choice Awards, including Favorite Male Music Performer for the last six years. He was named Artist of the '90s at the 1997 Blockbuster Entertainment Awards.

Given the past eight years of sales, awards and concert tickets, there is no doubt that the numbers connected to Garth Brooks are formidable.

TABLE OF CONTENTS

Against The Grain
Ropin' The Wind 146

Ain't Going Down ('Til The Sun Comes Up)
In Pieces 241

Alabama Clay
Garth Brooks 66

American Honky-Tonk Bar Association
In Pieces 280

Anonymous
In Pieces 286

The Beaches Of Cheyenne
Fresh Horses 296

Burning Bridges
Ropin' The Wind 141

Callin' Baton Rouge
In Pieces 256

The Change
Fresh Horses 300

Cold Shoulder
Ropin' The Wind 162

Cowboy Bill
Garth Brooks 70

The Cowboy Song
In Pieces 246

Cowboys And Angels
Fresh Horses 304

The Dance
Garth Brooks 73

Dixie Chicken
The Chase 192

Every Now And Then
The Chase 196

Everytime That It Rains
Garth Brooks 76

Face To Face
The Chase 210

The Fever
Fresh Horses 312

Friends In Low Places
No Fences 103

I Know One
Garth Brooks 79

If Tomorrow Never Comes
Garth Brooks 84

In Lonesome Dove
Ropin' The Wind 166

Ireland
Fresh Horses 307

It's Midnight Cinderella
Fresh Horses 318

I've Got A Good Thing Going
Garth Brooks 82

Kickin' And Screamin'
In Pieces 251

Learning To Live Again
The Chase 199

Mr. Blue
No Fences 106

Mr. Right
The Chase 202

Much Too Young (To Feel This Damn Old)
Garth Brooks 90

New Way To Fly
No Fences 112

The Night I Called The Old Man Out
In Pieces 262

Night Rider's Lament
The Chase 214

The Night Will Only Know
In Pieces 268

Nobody Gets Off In This Town
Garth Brooks 94

Not Counting You
Garth Brooks 87

The Old Stuff
Fresh Horses 326

One Night A Day
In Pieces 272

Papa Loved Mama
Ropin' The Wind 152

The Red Strokes
In Pieces 276

The River
Ropin' The Wind 157

Rodeo
Ropin' The Wind 170

Rollin'
Fresh Horses 333

Same Old Story
No Fences 109

Shameless
Ropin' The Wind 174

She's Every Woman
Fresh Horses 340

Something With A Ring To It
The Chase 205

Somewhere Other Than The Night
The Chase 220

Standing Outside The Fire
In Pieces 290

That Ol' Wind
Fresh Horses 345

That Summer
The Chase 226

This Ain't Tennessee
No Fences 116

The Thunder Rolls
No Fences 120

To Make You Feel My Love
Fresh Horses 322

Two Of A Kind, Workin' On A Full House
No Fences 124

Unanswered Prayers
No Fences 127

Uptown Down-Home Good Ol' Boy
Garth Brooks 98

Victim Of The Game
No Fences 132

Walking After Midnight
The Chase 236

We Bury The Hatchet
Ropin' The Wind 180

We Shall Be Free
The Chase 231

What She's Doing Now
Ropin' The Wind 184

Which One Of Them
Ropin' The Wind 188

Wild Horses
No Fences 138

Wolves
No Fences 135

Dan Roberts, Bryan Kennedy and I dedicate one
morning a year to a "sunrise ride."

On my horse, Crackerjack, in the middle of two
good friends, I was watching the sun come up over
the hay fields when Dan's voice broke the silence.
He asked me if I knew the difference between
grace and mercy. A smile came across Bryan's face.
Dan said, "Grace is when God gives us what we
don't deserve and mercy is when God doesn't give
us what we do deserve…" It made me think –
that pretty much wraps up my whole life.

God's grace and mercy on us all –

Not Counting You

I've Got A Good Thing Going

If Tomorrow Never Comes

Uptown Down-Home Good Ol' Boy

Everytime That It Rains

Alabama Clay

Much Too Young (To Feel This Damn Old)

Cowboy Bill

Nobody Gets Off In This Town

I Know One

The Dance

garth

This album is dedicated to the loving memories of
Jim Kelley and Heidi Miller

brooks

NOT COUNTING YOU
(Garth Brooks)

When loving turns to parting I'm always the first to leave
'Cause when it comes to heartaches I'd rather give than to receive
I've never cried myself to sleep just praying I'll get through
I've never lost at love not counting you

(Chorus)
Not counting you I've never had a heartache
Not counting you I never have been blue
There's no exceptions to the rule
I've never been nobody's fool
I've never lost at love not counting you

I've never got down on my knees and asked the Lord above
If he would only bring to me the one I'm dreaming of
Begging to be taken back and swearing I'll be true
Has never crossed my mind not counting you

(Repeat Chorus)

There's no exceptions to the rule
I've never been nobody's fool
I've never lost at love not counting you
No, I've never lost at love not counting you

I'VE GOT A GOOD THING GOING
(Larry Bastian, Sandy Mahl, Garth Brooks)

She swears there's nothing wrong, but something's missing
She's never been much good at telling lies
'Cause you can hear the sounds of leaving, if you listen
This may be California, but Oklahoma's in her eyes

(Chorus)
I've got a good thing going
It's plain to see, she's tired of hanging on
I've got a good thing going
It's killing me that she's as good as gone

By now she must be tired of always giving
And tired of what she's getting in return
I guess Oklahoma's more her style of living
'Cause I can see her heart is heading 'cross a bridge I thought she'd burned

(Repeat Chorus)

Lord it's killing me, that she's as good as gone

IF TOMORROW NEVER COMES
(Kent Blazy, Garth Brooks)

Sometimes late at night
I lie awake and watch her sleeping
She's lost in peaceful dreams
So I turn out the lights and lay there in the dark
And the thought crosses my mind
If I never wake up in the morning
Would she ever doubt the way I feel
About her in my heart

(Chorus)
If tomorrow never comes
Will she know how much I loved her
Did I try in every way to show her every day
That she's my only one
And if my time on earth were through
And she must face the world without me
Is the love I gave her in the past
Gonna be enough to last
If tomorrow never comes

'Cause I've lost loved ones in my life
Who never knew how much I loved them
Now I live with the regret
That my true feelings for them never were revealed
So I made a promise to myself
To say each day how much she means to me
And avoid that circumstance
Where there's no second chance to tell her how I feel

(Repeat Chorus)

So tell that someone that you love
Just what you're thinking of
If tomorrow never comes

UPTOWN DOWN-HOME GOOD OL' BOY
(DeWayne Blackwell, Earl Bud Lee)

He'll never wear a business suit
Cowboy hats and bull hide boots just suit him fine
See that buckle shine

He won it in a rodeo
On a horse named Desperado
And he won the ride but he broke his back
Hit so hard he heard it crack
No more rodeo

But you can't keep a good man down
A line of western wear uptown heard of his fame
And they bought his name

Now he looks down from a suite
At the silver limo parked out on the street
And he's not just a face in a martini crowd
He drinks long neck Bud and gets a little loud
The man's back on his feet

He's an uptown down-home good ol' boy
In a business world so fast
On a horse of a different color
But he'll hang on 'til the last
He's still the local hero
He's the hometown pride and joy
He's an uptown down-home good ol' boy

A woman loved him through it all
Through his rowdy days and his hardest fall when he almost died
She stayed by his side

She's still right there today
He wouldn't have it any other way
And he never did get too proud
To hang out with the same old crowd
We're proud to say

He's an uptown down-home good ol' boy
In a business world so fast
Oh but it's a different saddle
Than he once rode in the past
Well he's still the local hero
He's the hometown pride and joy
He's an uptown down-home good ol' boy
He's an uptown down-home good ol' boy

EVERYTIME THAT IT RAINS
(Charley Stefl, Ty England, Garth Brooks)

Stuck in an airport in Austin, all of the flights are delayed
And as the rain keeps fallin' the memories keep callin' me back
To another time and place
Back to a rainy day in Oklahoma, she was workin' at this roadside cafe
And it was just her and me and looked like it would be
At least 'til the storms rolled away

I played "Please Come to Boston" on the jukebox
She said hey that's my favorite song
The next thing I knew, the song was through
And we were still dancin' along
And with that look in her eyes she pulled from me

Then she pulled off that apron she wore
And with her hand in mine we turned off the sign
And locked the rain outside the door

(Chorus)
Every time that it rains, I can hear her heart callin'
It rains, I can see that dress fallin'
The storm clouds roll on, still the memory remains
Every time that it rains

One late rainy night I got a phone call
So I went back to see her again
And through the dance we both stumbled and with the buttons we fumbled
So we decided just to call it at friends
If we ever had a thing now it's over, and only the memory remains
Of a roadside cafe on a September day
I relive every time that it rains

(Repeat Chorus)

ALABAMA CLAY
(Larry Cordle, Ronny Scaife)

First time he saw the ground get busted
He was ten and it was 1952
His daddy worked hard from sunup to sundown
And the goin' got tough behind them ol' gray mules

The farm grew to be a moneymaker
And the house he lived in grew up room by room
The boy worked hard but soon got tired of farmin'
So he slipped away one night 'neath the harvest moon

(First Chorus)
His neck was red as Alabama clay
But the city's call pulled him away
He's got a factory job and runs a big machine
He don't miss the farm or the fields of green

(Instrumental Break)

Now the city's just a prison without fences
His job is just a routine he can't stand
And at night he dreams of wide-open spaces
Fresh dirt between his toes and on his hands

Then one day a picture came inside a letter
Of a young girl with a baby in her arms
And the words she wrote would change his life forever
So he went to raise his family on the farm

(Second Chorus)
His neck is red as Alabama clay
Now he's goin' home this time to stay
Where the roots run deep on the family tree
And the tractor rolls through the fields of green

(Repeat Second Chorus)

His neck is red as Alabama clay

MUCH TOO YOUNG (TO FEEL THIS DAMN OLD)
(Randy Taylor, Garth Brooks)

This ol' highway's getting longer
Seems there ain't no end in sight
To sleep would be best, but I just can't afford to rest
I've got to ride in Denver tomorrow night

I called the house but no one answered
For the last two weeks no one's been home
I guess she's through with me, to tell the truth I just can't see
What's kept the woman holding on this long

(Chorus)
And the white line's getting longer and the saddle's getting cold
I'm much too young to feel this damn old
All my cards are on the table and no ace left in the hole
I'm much too young to feel this damn old

The competition's getting younger
Tougher broncs, you know I can't recall

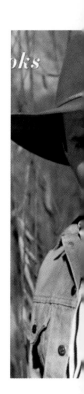

A worn out tape of Chris LeDoux, lonely women and bad booze
Seem to be the only friends I've left at all

(Repeat Chorus)

Lord, I'm much too young to feel this damn old

COWBOY BILL
(Larry Bastian, Ed Berghoff)

He told a good story and all of us kids listened
'Bout his life on the border and the way it was then
And we all believed him and when he would finish
We'd ask the old cowboy to tell 'em again

You could almost hear those prairie winds blowin'
His saddle a creakin' 'neath his old faded jeans
You could taste the dry dust from the trail he was ridin'
As he sat there and painted those west Texas scenes

(First Chorus)
And the grown-ups would tell us
You boys keep your distance, that old man's just tellin' you lies
But to all of us kids Cowboy Bill was a hero
Just as true as his blue Texas skies

He told of a time when he rode with the Rangers
Down on the pecos and he saved the day
Outnumbered by plenty, they were almost too cover
With thirty banditos headed their way

He looked back just in time to see a horse stumble
The captain went down and Bill pulled up on his reins
And through a flurry of bullets he rescued the captain
They rode for a sunset, just the story remains

(Repeat First Chorus)

Well I still remember the day that it happened
We waited and we waited but Bill never showed
And the folks at the feed store said they hadn't seen him
So we set out for his place down Old Grist Mill Road

And we cried when we found him lying there with his memories
The old trunk wide open, things scattered about
He was clutchin' a badge that said Texas Ranger
And an old "yeller" letter said Texas Is Proud

(Second Chorus)
And the grown-ups that told us
You boys keep your distance, that old man's just tellin' you lies
Well now they're all sayin' Cowboy Bill was a hero
Just as true as his blue Texas skies

Just as true as his blue Texas skies

NOBODY GETS OFF IN THIS TOWN
(Larry Bastian, DeWayne Blackwell)

Nobody gets off in this town
Trains don't even slow down
My high school sweetheart's married and gone
They met on a bus to San Antone
The Greyhound stops! Somebody gets on
But nobody gets off in this town

Nobody gets off in this town
Old folks 'round here wear a frown
Now let me see if I can set the scene
It's a one-dog town and he's old and mean
There's one stop light but it's always green
Nobody gets off in this town

Nobody gets off in this town
High school colors are brown
They can't drag Main because it kicks up dust
Their cars and their dreams are all starting to rust
The high school dances are always a bust
Nobody gets off in this town

Nobody gets off in this town
They oughta just tear it down
'Cause in the winter you freeze and in the summer you fry

Utility bill's the only thing that gets high
I'd go for a drink but this county is dry
Nobody gets off
Nobody gets off
Nobody gets off in this square old merry-go-round
No, nobody gets off in this town

I KNOW ONE
(Jack Clement)

When all your loves have ended
When all your friends have flown
Who'll be around to want you
When all your loves have gone

Only a fool would do it
After the way you've done
And how many fools would have you
I know one

This fool keeps wondering why he fell in love at all
But you might need this fool around in case you fall
After the party's over and you've had your fill of fun
If you need a fool to forgive you...I know one

You never know you might be lonely when all your loves have missed
It wouldn't hurt to keep an extra fool on your list
After your heart's been broken and you need a place to run
If you'll take a fool who loves you...I know one...I know one

THE DANCE
(Tony Arata)

Looking back on the memory of
The dance we shared 'neath the stars above
For a moment all the world was right
How could I have known that you'd ever say goodbye

(Chorus)
And now I'm glad I don't know
The way it all would end the way it all would go
Our lives are better left to chance I could have missed the pain
But I'd of had to miss the dance

Holding you I held everything
For a moment wasn't I a king
But if I'd only known how the King would fall
Hey who's to say you know I might have changed it all

(Repeat Chorus)

Yes my life is better left to chance
I could have missed the pain but I'd of had to miss the dance

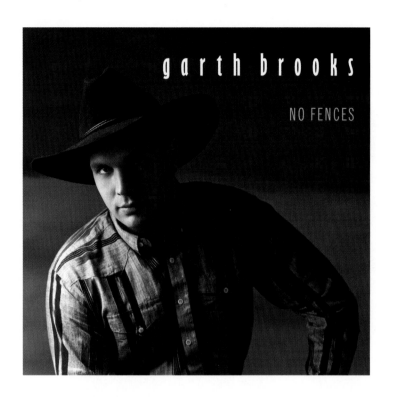

THE THUNDER ROLLS

NEW WAY TO FLY

TWO OF A KIND, WORKIN' ON A FULL HOUSE

VICTIM OF THE GAME

FRIENDS IN LOW PLACES

THIS AIN'T TENNESSEE

WILD HORSES

UNANSWERED PRAYERS

SAME OLD STORY

MR. BLUE

WOLVES

This album is dedicated to all who hear the music
and have the courage to dance.

F E N C E S

THE THUNDER ROLLS

(Pat Alger, Garth Brooks)

Three thirty in the morning
Not a soul in sight
The city's lookin' like a ghost town
On a moonless summer night
Raindrops on the windshield
There's a storm moving in
He's headin' back from somewhere
That he never should have been
And the thunder rolls
And the thunder rolls

Every light is burnin'
In a house across town
She's pacin' by the telephone
In her faded flannel gown
Askin' for a miracle
Hopin' she's not right
Prayin' its the weather
That's kept him out all night
And the thunder rolls
And the thunder rolls

(Chorus)
The thunder rolls
And the lightnin' strikes
Another love grows cold
On a sleepless night
As the storm blows on
Out of control
Deep in her heart
The thunder rolls

She's waitin' by the window
When he pulls into the drive
She rushes out to hold him
Thankful he's alive
But on the wind and rain
A strange new perfume blows
And the lightnin' flashes in her eyes
And he knows that she knows
And the thunder rolls
And the thunder rolls

(Repeat Chorus)

NEW WAY TO FLY

(Kim Williams, Garth Brooks)

Like birds on a high line
They line up at night time at the bar
They all once were lovebirds
Now bluebirds are all that they are
They landed in hell
The minute they fell from love's sky
And now they hope in the wine
That they'll find a new way to fly

(Chorus)
A new way to fly
Far away from goodbye
Above the clouds and the rain
The memories and the pain
And the tears that they cry
Now the lesson's been learned
They've all crashed and burned
But they can leave it behind
If they could just find
A new way to fly

By the end of the night
They'll be high as a kite once again
And they don't seem to mind all the time
Or the money they spend
It's a high price to pay
To just find a way to get by
But it's worth every dime
If they find a new way to fly

(Repeat Chorus)

They'll leave it behind
As soon as they find
A new way to fly

TWO OF A KIND, WORKIN' ON A FULL HOUSE

(Bobby Boyd, Warren Dale Haynes, Dennis Robbins)
(Thanks John!)

Yea, she's my lady luck
Hey, I'm her wild card man
Together we're buildin' up a real hot hand
We live out in the country
Hey, she's my little queen of the south
Yea, we're two of a kind
Workin' on a full house

She wakes me every mornin'
With a smile and a kiss
Her strong country lovin' is hard to resist
She's my easy lovin' woman
I'm her hard-workin' man, no doubt
Yea, we're two of a kind
Workin' on a full house

Yea, a pickup truck is her limousine
And her favorite dress is her faded blue jeans
She loves me tender when the goin' gets tough
Sometimes we fight just so we can make up

Lord I need that little woman
Like the crops need the rain
She's my honeycomb and I'm her sugar cane
We really fit together
If you know what I'm talkin' about
Yea, we're two of a kind
Workin' on a full house

This time I found a keeper, I made up my mind
Lord the perfect combination is her heart and mine
The sky's the limit, no hill is too steep
We're playin' for fun, but we're playin' for keeps

So draw the curtain, honey
Turn the lights down low
We'll find some country music on the radio
I'm yours and you're mine
Hey, that's what it's all about
Yea, we're two of a kind
Workin' on a full house

Lordy, mama, we'll be two of a kind
Workin' on a full house

VICTIM OF THE GAME

(Mark D. Sanders, Garth Brooks)

Well, it took a little time
But I guess you finally learned
That promises get broken
And bridges do get burned
You've been siftin' through the ashes
Just tryin' to find a flame
Holdin' on to nothin'
You're a victim of the game

You were standin' way too close
To see it all fall apart
And there were things you couldn't hear

'Cause you were listenin' with your heart
But you can't say I didn't warn you
Now there's no one else to blame
There's no one quite as blind
As a victim of the game

(Chorus)
And it don't matter who you are
It treats everyone the same
All you need's a heart
To be a victim of the game

You know it's really gettin' to you
When you take to tellin' lies
And you can try to fool your friends
But you can't look 'em in the eye
There ain't no standin' tall
In the shadow of the shame
When everybody knows
That you're a victim of the game

(Repeat Chorus)

Oh, you know, when I look into your eyes
I can really feel the pain
Starin' in the mirror
At a victim of the game

FRIENDS IN LOW PLACES
(DeWayne Blackwell, Earl Bud Lee)

Blame it all on my roots
I showed up in boots
And ruined your black tie affair
The last one to know
The last one to show
I was the last one
You thought you'd see there
And I saw the surprise
And the fear in his eyes
When I took his glass of champagne
And I toasted you
Said, honey, we may be through
But you'll never hear me complain

(Chorus)
'Cause I've got friends in low places
Where the whiskey drowns
And the beer chases my blues away
And I'll be okay
I'm not big on social graces
Think I'll slip on down to the oasis
Oh I've got friends in low places

Well, I guess I was wrong
I just don't belong
But then, I've been there before
Everything's all right
I'll just say goodnight
And I'll show myself to the door
Hey, I didn't mean
To cause a big scene
Just give me an hour and then
Well, I'll be as high
As that ivory tower
That you're livin' in

(Repeat Chorus)

THIS AIN'T TENNESSEE
(James Shaw, Larry Bastian)

It's a big estate
With wrought iron gates
And palm trees standin' tall
Fancy mirrors and chandeliers
Comfort wall to wall
And the ocean air is so crisp and clear
And they rave about our view

But there ain't no mountain breeze
And there ain't no hickory trees
And this ain't Tennessee
And she ain't you

There's a bedroom suite
Where she comes to me
And as her fingers touch my face
I close my eyes and I fantasize
Of another time and place
What she feels is so warm and real
And I know her love is true
And she tries so hard to please
Still I think sometimes she sees
That this ain't Tennessee
And she ain't you

It's not that it's not good enough
And it's not that I'm not man enough
There's just somethin' easy goin' that I love
About you and Tennessee

So I made up my mind to learn my lines
And try to play the part
But part of me is in Tennessee
And deep down in my heart
I miss my Smoky Mountain home
And I miss your lovin' too
And it's deep inside of me
And it's always gonna be
'Cause this ain't Tennessee
And she ain't you

WILD HORSES
(Bill Shore, David Wills)

From a phone booth in Cheyenne
I made a promise to Diane
No more rodeos
I'd gone my last go 'round

The same promise that I made
In San Antone and Santa Fe
But tonight I saddled up
And let her down

(Chorus)
Wild horses keep draggin' me away
And I'll lose more than I'm gonna win someday
Wild horses just stay wild
And her heart is all I break
Wild horses keep draggin' me away

She'll watch me drive around her block
Gettin' courage up to stop
To make her one more promise
That I can't keep

The way I love the rodeo
I guess I should let her go
Before I hurt her more
Than she loves me

(Repeat Chorus Twice)

UNANSWERED PRAYERS
(Pat Alger, Larry B. Bastian, Garth Brooks)

Just the other night at a hometown football game
My wife and I ran into my old high school flame
And as I introduced them the past came back to me
And I couldn't help but think of the way things used to be

She was the one that I'd wanted for all times
And each night I'd spend prayin' that God would make her mine
And if he'd only grant me this wish I wished back then
I'd never ask for anything again

(Chorus)
Sometimes I thank God for unanswered prayers
Remember when you're talkin' to the man upstairs

That just because he doesn't answer doesn't mean he don't care
Some of God's greatest gifts are unanswered prayers

She wasn't quite the angel that I remembered in my dreams
And I could tell that time had changed me
In her eyes too it seemed
We tried to talk about the old days
There wasn't much we could recall
I guess the Lord knows what he's doin' after all

And as she walked away and I looked at my wife
And then and there I thanked the Good Lord
For the gifts in my life

Sometimes I thank God for unanswered prayers
Remember when you're talkin' to the man upstairs
That just because he may not answer doesn't mean he don't care
Some of God's greatest gifts are unanswered . . .
Some of God's greatest gifts are all to often unanswered . . .
Some of God's greatest gifts are unanswered prayers

SAME OLD STORY
(Tony Arata)

While they dance
How she holds him
Pulls him close
And loves him so
While he dreams of another
And counts the days
Until he lets her go

Same old story
That everybody knows
It's one heart holdin' on
One letting go

While they ride
Lord, he tells her
How they two
Will settle down
But she only hears the highway
And a voice
In some other town

And the harder
He holds her
The more she slips away

Same old story
That everybody knows
It's one heart holdin' on
And one letting go
Same old story

MR. BLUE
(DeWayne Blackwell)

Our guardian star lost all its glow
The day that I lost you
It lost all its glitter the day you said "no"
And its grey skies turned to blue

Like him I am doubtful
That your love is true
So if you decide to call on me
Ask for Mr. Blue

I'm Mr. Blue
When you say you love me
Then prove it by goin' out on the sly
Provin' your love is untrue
Call me Mr. Blue

I'm Mr. Blue
When you say you're sorry
Then turn around headed for the lights of town
Hurtin' me through and through
Call me Mr. Blue

rook
NO FENC

I sleep alone each night
Wait by the phone each night
But you don't call
And I won't hurt my pride
Call me mister

I won't tell you
When you paint the town
A bright red to turn it upside down
I'm painting it too
But I'm painting it blue

I sleep alone each night
Wait by the phone each night
But you don't call
And I won't hurt my pride
Call me mister

I won't tell you
When you paint the town
A bright red to turn it upside down
I'm painting it too
But I'm painting it blue
Call me Mr. Blue
Call me mister

WOLVES
(Stephanie Davis)

January's always bitter
But Lord, this one beats all
The wind ain't quit for weeks now
And the drifts are ten feet tall
I been all night drivin' heifers
Closer in to lower ground
Then I spent the mornin' thinkin'
'Bout the ones the wolves pulled down

Charlie Barton and his family
Stopped today to say goodbye
He said the bank was takin' over
The last few years were just too dry
And I promised that I'd visit
When they found a place in town
Then I spent a long time thinkin'
'Bout the ones the wolves pull down

Lord, please shine a light of hope
On those of us who fall behind
And when we stumble in the snow
Could you help us up while there's still time

Well, I don't mean to be complainin' Lord
You've always seen me through
And I know you got your reasons
For each and every thing you do
But tonight outside my window
There's a lonesome, mournful sound
And I just can't keep from thinkin'
'Bout the ones the wolves pull down

Oh Lord, keep me from bein'
The one the wolves pull down

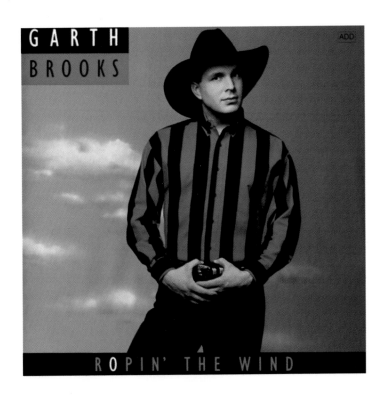

AGAINST THE GRAIN

RODEO

WHAT SHE'S DOING NOW

BURNING BRIDGES

WHICH ONE OF THEM

PAPA LOVED MAMA

SHAMELESS

COLD SHOULDER

WE BURY THE HATCHET

IN LONESOME DOVE

THE RIVER

R O P I N '

This album is dedicated to Reba's "Crazy Eight", to
their families and friends. I wish God's strength and
understanding upon you

THE WIND

AGAINST THE GRAIN
(Bruce Bouton, Larry Cordle, Carl Jackson)

Folks call me a maverick
Guess I ain't too diplomatic
I just never been the kind to go along
Just avoidin' confrontation
For the sake of conformation
And I'll admit I tend to sing a different song
But sometimes you just can't be afraid
To wear a different hat
If Columbus had complied
This old world might still be flat
Nothin' ventured, nothin' gained
Sometimes you've got to go against the grain

Well, I have been accused
Of makin' my own rules
There must be rebel blood
Just a-runnin' through my veins
But I ain't no hypocrite
What you see is what you get
And that's the only way I know
To play the game
Old Noah took much ridicule
For building his great ark
But after forty days and forty nights
He was lookin' pretty smart
Sometimes it's best to brave the wind and rain
By havin' strength to go against the grain

Well, there's more folks than a few
Who share my point of view
But they're worried
If they're gonna sink or swim
They'd like to buck the system
But the deck is stacked against 'em
And they're a little scared
To go out on a limb
But if you're gonna make a difference
If you're gonna leave your mark
You can't follow like a bunch of sheep
You got to listen to your heart
Go bustin' in like old John Wayne
Sometimes you got to go against the grain

Nothin' ventured, nothin' gained
Sometimes you've got to go against the grain

RODEO
(Larry Bastian)

His eyes are cold and restless
His wounds have almost healed
And she'd give half of Texas
Just to change the way he feels
She knows his love's in Tulsa
And she knows he's gonna go
Well, it ain't no woman, flesh and blood
It's that damned old rodeo

(Chorus)
Well, it's bulls and blood
It's dust and mud
It's the roar of a Sunday crowd
It's the white in his knuckles
The gold in the buckle
He'll win the next go 'round
It's boots and chaps
It's cowboy hats

It's spurs and latigo
It's the ropes and the reins
And the joy and the pain
And they call the thing rodeo

She does her best to hold him
When his love comes to call
But his need for it controls him
And her back's against the wall
And it's "So long girl, I'll see you"
When it's time for him to go
You know the woman wants her cowboy
Like he wants his rodeo

(Repeat Chorus)

It'll drive a cowboy crazy
It'll drive the man insane
And he'll sell off everything he owns
Just to pay to play her game
And a broken home and some broken bones
Is all he'll have to show
For all the years that he spent chasin'
This dream they call rodeo

(Repeat Chorus)

It's the broncs and the blood
It's the steers and the mud
And they call the thing rodeo

WHAT SHE'S DOING NOW
(Pat Alger, Garth Brooks)

Last time I saw her it was turnin' colder
But that was years ago
Last I heard she had moved to Boulder
But where she's now, I don't know
But there's somethin' 'bout this time of year
That spins my head around
Takes me back, makes me wonder
What's she doin' now

(Chorus)
'Cause what she's doin' now is tearin' me apart
Fillin' up my mind and emptying my heart
I can hear her call each time the cold wind blows
And I wonder if she knows…what she's doin' now

Just for laughs, I dialed her old number
But no one knew her name
Hung up the phone, sat there and wondered
If she'd ever done the same
I took a walk in the evenin' wind
To clear my head somehow
But tonight I lie here thinkin'
What's she doin' now

(Repeat Chorus Twice)

BURNING BRIDGES
(Stephanie C. Brown, Garth Brooks)

Yesterday she thanked me
For oilin' that front door
This morning when she wakes
She won't be thankful anymore
She'll never know how much I cared
Just that I couldn't stay
And I'll never know the reason
Why I always run away

(Chorus)
Burning bridges one by one
What I'm doin' can't be undone
And I'm always hoping someday
I'm gonna stop this runnin' around
But every time the chance comes up
Another bridge goes down

Last night we talked of old times
Families and home towns
She wondered if we'd both agree
On where we'd settle down
And I told her that we'd cross that bridge
Whenever it arrived
Now through the flames I see her
Standin' on the other side

(Repeat Chorus)

Like ashes on the water
I drift away in sorrow
Knowing that the day
My lesson's finally learned
I'll be standing at a river
Staring out across tomorrow
And the bridge I need to get there
Will be a bridge that I have burned

(Repeat Chorus)

Another bridge goes down

WHICH ONE OF THEM
(Garth Brooks)

The girl at the bar, she bought me a beer
And she'd like to know if I'm new around here
And the gal that I danced with says she's all alone
Her friends have all left and she needs a ride home

Oh and there have been others who gave me the eye
But if they only knew they were wasting their time
'Cause there's only one lover I can give my heart to
But you didn't' want it and you broke it in two

(Chorus)
(So tell me) which one of them will be you tonight
Oh which one will hold me in your arms so tight
I've forgotten what's wrong, given up on what's right
(Tell me) which one of them will be you tonight

So I'll just smile and pretend and she'll never know
Who she's up against when she's holdin' me close
You're all that I want, girl, you're all that I need
And when I close my eyes, honey you're all I see

(Repeat Chorus)

PAPA LOVED MAMA
(Kim Williams, Garth Brooks)

Papa drove a truck nearly all his life
You know it drove Mama crazy being a trucker's wife
The part she couldn't handle was the being alone
I guess she needed more to hold than just a telephone
Papa called Mama each and every night
Just to ask her how she was and if us kids were all right
Mama would wait for that call to come in
When Daddy'd hang up she was gone again

(Chorus)
Mama was a looker
Lord, how she shined
Papa was a good'n
But the jealous kind
Papa loved Mama
Mama loved men
Mama's in the graveyard
Papa's in the pen

Well, it was bound to happen and one night it did
Papa came home and it was just us kids
He had a dozen roses and bottle of wine
If he was lookin' to surprise us, he was doin' fine
I heard him cry for Mama up and down the hall
Then I heard a bottle break against the bedroom wall
That old diesel engine made an eerie sound
When Papa fired it up and headed into town

Well, the picture in the paper showed the scene real well
Papa's rig was buried in the local motel
The desk clerk said he saw it all real clear
He never hit the breaks and he was shifting gears

(Repeat Chorus)

SHAMELESS

(Billy Joel)

Well I'm shameless when it comes to loving you
I'll do anything you want me to
I'll do anything at all

And I'm standing here for all the world to see
Oh baby, that's what's left of me
Don't have very far to fall

You know now I'm not a man who has ever been
Insecure about the world I've been living in
I don't break easy, I have my pride
But if you need to be satisfied

I'm shameless, oh honey, I don't have a prayer
Every time I see you standin' there
I go down upon my knees
And I'm changing, swore I'd never compromise
Oh, but you convinced me otherwise
I'll do anything you please

You see in all my life I've never found
What I couldn't resist, what I couldn't turn down
I could walk away from anyone I ever knew
But I can't walk away from you

I never let anything have this much control over me
I work too hard to call my life my own
And I've made myself a world and it's worked so perfectly
But it's your world now, I can't refuse
I've never had so much to lose
Oh, I'm shameless

You know it should be easy for a man who's strong
To say he's sorry or admit when he's wrong
I've never lost anything I've ever missed
But I've never been in love like this

It's out of my hands

I'm shameless, I don't have the power now
I don't want it anyhow
So I got to let it go

Oh, I'm shameless, shameless as a man can be
You can make a total fool of me
I just wanted you to know

Oh, I'm shameless, I just wanted you to know
Oh, I'm shameless, Oh, I'm down on my knees…shameless

COLD SHOULDER

(Kent Blazy, Kim Williams, Garth Brooks)

There's a fire burning bright
At our house tonight
Slow music playing
And soft candlelight
On her lips I keep tasting
The warm red wine
I'm there in her arms
But it's all in my mind

(Chorus)
The snow is piled high on the highway tonight
I'm a ship lost at sea on this ocean of white
Eighteen wheels anchored somewhere out of Dover
I wish I could hold her
Instead of huggin' this old cold shoulder

This old highway
Is like a woman sometimes

She can be your best friend
But she's the real jealous kind
She's the lady that leads me
To the life I dream of
She's the mistress that keeps me
From the ones that I love

(Repeat Chorus)

God, I wish I could hold her
Instead of huggin' this old cold shoulder

WE BURY THE HATCHET
(Wade Kimes, Garth Brooks)

Hey, all the neighbors' lights
Came on last night
Just like they do every time
We have a little fight
It's gettin' to the point
We can't get along
We're always fighting about things
That should be dead and gone

(Chorus)
We bury the hatchet
But leave the handle stickin' out
We're always diggin' up things
We should forget about
When it comes to forgivin'
Baby, there ain't no doubt
We bury the hatchet
But leave the handle sticking out

Well, I was kissing on Cindy
Hey, that I won't deny
But that's a long time ago
I let a dead dog lie
But if you want to cut deep
How 'bout you and ol' Joe
I caught you down at the creek
Just ten years ago

(Repeat Chorus)

Hey, we got enough on each other
To wage a full scale war
If we could ever remember
What we were fightin' for

(Repeat Chorus)

We bury the hatchet
But leave the handle stickin' out

IN LONESOME DOVE
(Cynthia Limbaugh, Garth Brooks)

She was a girl on a wagon train
Headed west across the plains
The train got lost in a summer storm
They couldn't move west and they couldn't go home
Then she saw him ridin' through the rain
He took charge of the wagons and he saved the train
And she looked down and her heart was gone
The train went west but she stayed on
In Lonesome Dove

A farmer's daughter with a gentle hand
A blooming rose in a bed of sand
She loved the man who wore a star
A Texas Ranger known near and far
So they got married and they had a child
But times were tough and the West was wild
So it was no surprise the day she learned
That her Texas man would not return
To Lonesome Dove

Chorus)
Back to back with the Rio Grande
A Christian woman in the devil's land
She learned the language and she learned to fight
But she never learned how to beat the lonely nights
In Lonesome Dove, Lonesome Dove

She watched her boy grow to a man
He had an angel's heart and the devil's hand
He wore his star for all to see
He was a Texas lawman legacy
Then one day word blew into town
It seemed the men that shot his father down
Had robbed a bank in Cherico
The only thing 'tween them and Mexico
Was Lonesome Dove

The shadows stretched across the land
As the shots rang out down the Rio Grande
And when the smoke had finally cleared the street
The men lay at the ranger's feet
But legend tells to this very day
That shots were comin' from an alleyway
'Though no one knows who held the gun
There ain't no doubt if you ask someone
In Lonesome Dove

(Repeat Chorus)

THE RIVER
(Victoria Shaw, Garth Brooks)

You know a dream is like a river
Ever changin' as it flows
And a dreamer's just a vessel
That must follow where it goes
Trying to learn from what's behind you
And never knowing what's in store
Makes each day a constant battle
Just to stay between the shores . . . and

(Chorus)
I will sail my vessel
'Til the river runs dry
Like a bird upon the wind
These waters are my sky
I'll never reach my destination
If I never try
So I will sail my vessel
'Til the river runs dry

Too many times we stand aside
And let the waters slip away
'Til what we put off 'til tomorrow
Has now become today
So don't you sit upon the shoreline
And say you're satisfied
Choose to chance the rapids
And dare to dance the tide . . . yes

(Repeat Chorus)

And there's bound to be rough waters
And I know I'll take some falls
But with the good Lord as my captain
I can make it through them all . . . yes

(Repeat Chorus)

Yes, I will sail my vessel
'Til the river runs dry
'Til the river runs dry

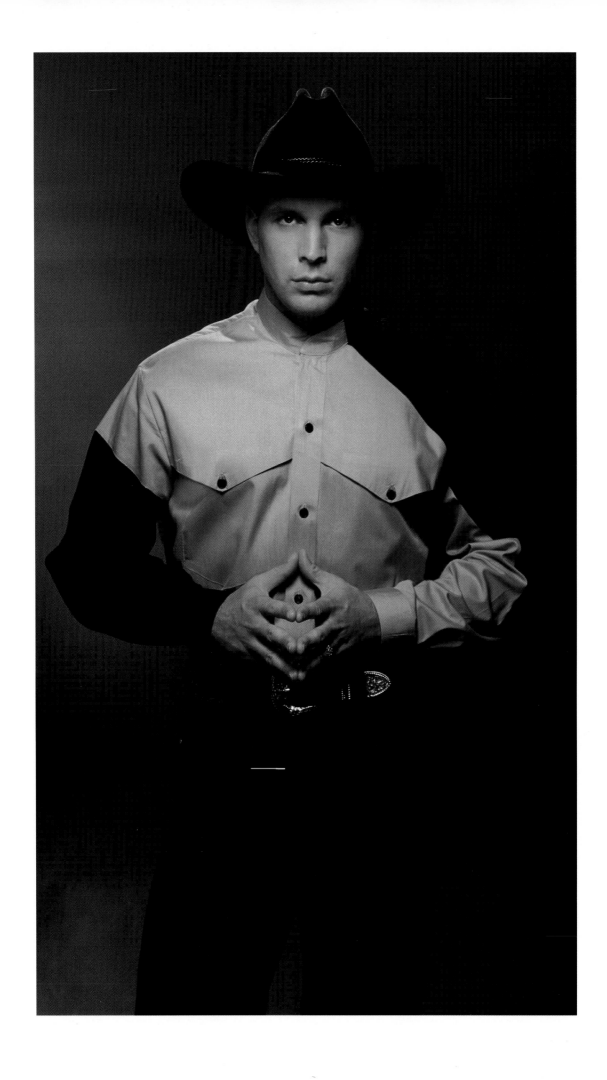

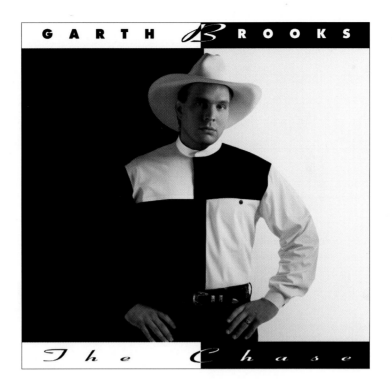

We Shall Be Free

Somewhere Other Than The Night

Mr. Right

Every Now And Then

Walking After Midnight

Dixie Chicken

Learning To Live Again

That Summer

Something With A Ring To It

Night Rider's Lament

Face To Face

The

This album is dedicated to Dale Wehr . . . I will always remember what you taught me about building barns, hauling hay, and horses. What I will remember most, however, I'm not sure you intended to teach me. Those who fear death are the same ones who have not lived their lives to the fullest; when you laughed in death's face, you were not being courageous, you were just being honest. I miss you pal and that shit-eatin' grin of yours.

Chase

WE SHALL BE FREE
(Stephanie Davis, Garth Brooks)

This ain't comin' from no prophet
Just an ordinary man
When I close my eyes I see
The way this world shall be
When we all walk hand in hand

When the last child cries for a crust of bread
When the last man dies for just words that he said
When there's shelter over the poorest head
We shall be free

When the last thing we notice is the color of skin
And the first thing we look for is the beauty within
When the skies and the oceans are clean again
Then we shall be free

We shall be free
We shall be free
Stand straight, walk proud
'Cause we shall be free

When we're free to love anyone we choose
When this world's big enough for all different views
When we all can worship from our own kind of pew
Then we shall be free

We shall be free
We shall be free
Have a little faith
Hold out
'Cause we shall be free

And when money talks for the very last time
And nobody walks a step behind
When there's only one race and that's mankind
Then we shall be free

We shall be free
We shall be free
Stand straight, walk proud, have a little faith, hold out
We shall be free

We shall be free
We shall be free
Stand straight, have a little faith
We shall be free

We shall be free *(repeat 2 times)*

Background Vocals: D. Mc And Friends - Donna McElroy, Vicki Hampton, Yvonne Hodges, Debbie Nims, Gary Chapman, Howard Smith and Johnny Cobb

SOMEWHERE OTHER THAN THE NIGHT
(Kent Blazy, Garth Brooks)

He could see the storm clouds rollin' across the hill
He barely beat the rain in from the field
And between the backdoor slammin' she heard him say
"Damn this rain and damn this wasted day"
But she'd been waitin' for this day for oh so long
She was standin' in the kitchen with nothin' but her apron on
And in disbelief he stood and he stared a while
When their eyes met, they both began to smile

(Chorus)
Somewhere other than the night
She needs to hear I love you
Somewhere other than the night
She needs to know you care
She wants to know she's needed
She needs to be held tight
Somewhere other than the night

They spent the day wrapped up in a blanket
On the front porch swing
He'd come to realize he'd neglected certain things
And there are times she feels alone even by his side
It was the first time she ever saw him cry

(Repeat Chorus)

To know she's needed
She needs to be held tight
Somewhere other than the night

MR. RIGHT
(Garth Brooks)

I can tell by the way you've been turning men down
Not your ordinary guy is gonna do
You've been waitin' for that someone
Who can turn your head around
Well now honey, I'm that special one for you

(Chorus)
There must be a million fish out in that ocean
So you must find the one that's right for you somehow
Well, it's up to you , I'm here for years
Or 'till the night-time disappears
I'm Mr. Right or Mr. Right now

And if you'd choose to be my wife
I would love you all my life
I'd do everything your precious heart allowed
Or we could make love all night long
And in the morning I'd be gone
I'm Mr. Right or Mr. Right now

(Repeat Chorus)

I'm Mr. Right forever or just until whenever
Mr. Right or Mr. Right now

EVERY NOW AND THEN
(Buddy Mondlock, Garth Brooks)

I walked down to the park last night
Warm breeze stirring up a soft moonlight
And my mind started drifting to way back when
Yes I do think about you every now and then

The other day I saw a car like you used to drive
I got a funny feeling down deep inside
And for the briefest moment I felt a smile begin
Yes I do think about you every now and then

(Chorus)
I love my life and I'd never trade
Between what you and me had and the life I've made
She's here and she's real, but you were too
And every once in a while I think about you

I heard a song on the radio just yesterday
The same one you always asked me to play
And when the song was over
I wished they'd played it again
Yes I do think about you every now and then

(Repeat Chorus)

I've been layin' here all night listenin' to the rain
Talkin' to my heart and trying to explain
Why sometimes I catch myself
Wondering what might have been
Yes I do think about you every now and then
Every now and then
Every now and then

Background Vocal: Garth Brooks

WALKING AFTER MIDNIGHT
(Alan Block, Don Hecht)

I go out walkin' after midnight
Out in the starlight
Just like we used to do
I'm always walkin' after midnight
Searching for you

I walk for miles along the highway
Well, that's just my way
Of sayin' I love you
I'm always walkin' after midnight
Searchin' for you

I stop to see a weeping willow
Cryin' on his pillow
Maybe he's cryin' for me
And as the skies turn gloomy
Night winds whisper to me
I'm lonesome as I can be

I go out walkin' after midnight
Out in the moonlight
Just a - hopin' you may be
Somewhere a - walkin' after midnight
Searchin' for me

(Repeat last two verses)

I go out walkin' after midnight
Searchin' for you

DIXIE CHICKEN
(Lowell George, Martin Kibbee)

I seen the bright lights of Memphis
And the Commodore Hotel
And it was there beneath the street lamp
Where I met a southern belle
Well she took me to the river
Where she cast her spell
And it was 'neath that Memphis moonlight
She sang this song so well

(Chorus)
If you'll be my Dixie chicken
I'll be your Tennessee lamb
And we can walk together
Down in Dixie land
Down in Dixie land

We hit all the hot spots
My money flowed like wine
Till the lowdown southern whiskey
Began to fog my mind
Well I don't remember church bells
Or the money I put down
On the white picket fence and boardwalk
At the house on the edge of town
Now but boy do I remember
The strain of her refrain
And the nights we spent together
And the way she called by name

(Repeat Chorus)

It's been a year since she ran away
Guess that guitar player sure could play
She always liked to sing along
He was always handy with a song
Then one night in the lobby
Of the Commodore Hotel
I by chance met a bartender
Who said he knew her well
And as he handed me a drink
He began to hum a song
And all the boys there at the bar
Began to sing along

(Repeat Chorus Twice)

Background Vocals: Trisha Yearwood, Donna McElroy, Vicki Hampton, Yvonne Hodges, Debbie Nims

LEARNING TO LIVE AGAIN
(Don Schlitz, Stephanie Davis)

I burned my hand, and I cut my face
Heaven knows how long it's been
Since I've felt so out of place
I'm wonderin' if I'll fit in

Debbie and Charley said they'd be here by nine
And Deb said she might bring a friend
Just my luck, they're right on time
So here I go again

(Chorus)
I'm gonna smile my best smile
And I'm gonna laugh like it's goin' out of style
Look into her eyes and pray that she don't see
That learning to live again is killing me

Little cafe, table for four
But there's just conversation for three
I like the way she let me get the door
I wonder what she thinks of me

Debbie just whispered, "You're doin' fine"
And I wish that I felt the same
She's asked me to dance, now her hand's in mine
Oh, my god, I've forgotten her name

But I'm gonna smile my best smile
And I'm gonna laugh like it's goin' out of style
Look into her eyes and pray that she don't see
This learning to live again is killing me

Now here we are beneath her porch light
And I say what a great time it's been
A kiss on the cheek, a whisper goodnight
And I say "Can I see you again"

And she just smiles her best smile
And she laughs like it's goin' out of style
Looks into my eyes and says, "We'll see"
Oh this learning to live again is killing me
God this learning to live again is killing me

THAT SUMMER
(Pat Alger, Sandy Mahl, Garth Brooks)

I went to work for her that summer
A teenage kid so far from home
She was a lonely widow woman
Hell bent to make it on her own
We were a thousand miles from nowhere
Wheat fields as far as I could see
Both needin' somethin' from each other
Not knowin' yet what that might be

'Till she came to me one evening
Hot cup of coffee and a smile
In a dress that I was certain
She hadn't worn in quite a while
There was a difference in her laughter
There was a softness in her eyes
And on the air there was a hunger
Even a boy could recognize

(Chorus)
She had a need to feel the thunder
To chase the lightnin' from the skies
To watch the storm with all its wonder
Raging in her lover's eyes
She had to ride the heat of passion
Like a comet burnin' bright
Rushing head long in the wind
Out where only dreams had been
Burnin' both ends of the night

That summer wind was all around me
Nothin' between us but the night
And when I told her that I'd never
She softly whispered that's alright
And then I watched her hands of leather
Turn to velvet in a touch

There's never been another summer
When I have ever learned so much

(Repeat Chorus) (We)

I often think about that summer
The sweat the moonlight and the lace
And I have rarely held another
When I haven't seen her face
And every time I pass a wheat field
Watch it dancin' with the wind
Although I know it isn't real
I just can't help but feel
Her hungry arms again

(Repeat Chorus)

Rushing head long in the wind
Out where only dreams had been
Burnin' both ends of the night

Harmony: Trisha Yearwood

SOMETHING WITH A RING TO IT
(Aaron Tippin, Mark Collie)

(Chorus)
She wants something with a ring to it
Like a church bell makes
Like a pretty white gown to wear
And some vows to take
She wants something with a ring to it
I think I understand
Gonna have to put a ring on her finger
If I'm gonna be her man

My baby's playin' hard to please
And I think I figured out
What it is she wants from me
'Cause when I hold her close
When we go out at night
I can hardly see the moonlight
For the diamonds in her eyes

(Repeat Chorus)

My baby did but now she don't
And if I don't say I do
It's a safe bet that she won't
Love me like she used to
When our love first began
Now the only way to change her tune
Is with a wedding band

(Repeat Chorus)

Harmony: Garth Brooks

NIGHT RIDER'S LAMENT
(Michael Burton)

One night while I was out a ridin'
The grave yard shift, midnight 'til dawn
The moon was bright as a readin' light
For a letter from an old friend back home

And he asked me
Why do you ride for your money
Tell me why do you rope for short pay
You ain't a'gettin' nowhere
And you're loosin' your share
Boy, you must have gone crazy out there

He said last night I ran on to Jenny
She's married and has a good life
And boy you sure missed the track
When you never came back
She's the perfect professional's wife

And she asked me
Why does he ride for his money
And tell me why does he rope for short pay
He ain't a'gettin' nowhere

And he's loosin' his share
Boy he must've gone crazy out there

Ah but they've never seen the Northern Lights
They've never seen a hawk on the wing
They've never spent spring at the Great Divide
And they've never heard ole' camp cookie sing

Well I read up the last of my letter
And I tore off the stamp for black Jim
And when Billy rode up to relieve me
He just looked at my letter and grinned

He said now
Why do they ride for their money
Tell me why do they ride for short pay
They ain't a'gettin' nowhere
And they're losin' their share
Boy, they must have gone crazy out there
Son, they all must be crazy out there

Harmony: Trisha Yearwood and Garth Brooks

FACE TO FACE
(Tony Arata)

There was a bad boy in the school yard
Waited on you every day
Seemed like every time you turned around
Well he was standin' in your way

Well he broke your glasses
The girls all laughed
As he pushed you to the floor
But then you stood up one day knowin'
You couldn't stand it anymore
And your gentle hand was finally clenched in rage
You were face to face

(First Chorus)
Face to face with the devil that you've been dreadin'
Eye to eye finally has arrived
But bad as it was, well now brother wasn't it better
Dealin' with him face to face

Your date showed up with flowers
And you thought your dreams had come
But with every passing hour
You felt it come undone
Then the night exploded and you begged him no
But he forever changed your life
And now he waits a judge and jury
Thinkin' you'll break down inside
And with a finger you can put his fists away
And you're face to face

(Second Chorus)
Face to face with the devil that you've been dreadin'
Eye to eye finally has arrived
But bad as it was, well little sister wasn't it better
Dealin' with him face to face

'Cause it'll never go away
Until the fear that you are runnin' from is finally embraced
Drivin' by the graveyard
On a wicked winter's eve
And you're wonderin' why a man of faith
Is whistlin' nervously
Then you stop the car
And you hold your heart
'Cause you finally realize
Hell, the devil ain't in the darkness
He's a'rattlin' 'round inside
And with folded hands you truly start to pray
And you're face to face

(Repeat First Chorus)

'Cause it'll never go away
Until the fear that you are runnin' from is finally embraced
Face to face

G A

STANDING OUTSIDE THE FIRE

THE NIGHT I CALLED THE OLD MAN OUT

AMERICAN HONKY-TONK BAR ASSOCIATION

ONE NIGHT A DAY

KICKIN' AND SCREAMIN'

ANONYMOUS

AIN'T GOING DOWN ('TIL THE SUN COMES UP)

THE RED STROKES

CALLIN' BATON ROUGE

THE NIGHT WILL ONLY KNOW

THE COWBOY SONG

I N

PIECES

STANDING OUTSIDE THE FIRE
(Jenny Yates, Garth Brooks)

We call them cool
Those hearts that have no scars to show
The ones that never do let go
And risk the tables being turned

We call them fools
Who have to dance within the flame
Who chance the sorrow and the shame
That always comes with getting burned

But you got to be tough when consumed by desire
'Cause it's not enough just to stand outside the fire

We call them strong
Those who can face this world alone
Who seem to get by on their own
Those who will never take the fall

We call them weak
Who are unable to resist
The slightest chance love might exist
And for that forsake it all

They're so hell bent on giving, walking a wire
Convinced it's not living if you stand outside the fire

Chorus:
Standing outside the fire
Standing outside the fire
Life is not tried it is merely survived
If you're standing outside the fire

There's this love that is burning
Deep in my soul
Constantly yearning to get out of control
Wanting to fly higher and higher
I can't abide standing outside the fire

Repeat Chorus (twice)

Harmony: Trisha Yearwood, Garth Brooks

THE NIGHT I CALLED THE OLD MAN OUT
(Pat Alger, Kim Williams, Garth Brooks)

The dining room fell silent
I can't believe what I just said
I just told my dad he's full of it
And I watched his face turn red
And I should've said, "I'm sorry"
But I matched him shout for shout
I can still hear that screen door slammin'
The night I called him out

(Chorus)
He said, "Son, it's gonna hurt me more than it hurts you"
But somehow I couldn't help but have my doubts
'Cause I'd seen my older brothers crawl back in the house
Each time they called the old man out

Fist to fist and eye to eye
Standin' toe to toe
He would've let me walk away
But I just would not let it go
Years of my frustration
Had lead me to this night
Now he'll pay for all the times that he's been right

(Repeat Chorus)

It was over in a minute
That's when I realized

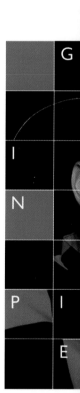

The blood came from my mouth and nose
But the tears came from his eyes
And in memory of that fateful night
I know the greatest pain was his
And I just pray someday I'm half the man he is

(Repeat Chorus)

Just like my older brothers
I crawled back in the house
The night I called the old man out

Harmony: Trisha Yearwood, Garth Brooks

AMERICAN HONKY-TONK BAR ASSOCIATION
(Bryan Kennedy, Jim Rushing)

If your paycheck depends on
The weather and the clock
If your conversation calls for
A little more than a coffee pot
If you need to pour your heart out
And try to rectify some situation
That you're facin'
Contact your American Honky-Tonk Bar Association

When Uncle Sam dips in your pocket
For most things you don't mind
But when your dollar goes to all of those
Standing in a welfare line
Rejoice you have a voice
If you're concerned about the destination
Of this great nation
It's called the American Honky-Tonk Bar Association

(Chorus)
It represents the hard-hat
Gunrack, achin'-back
Over-taxed, flag-wavin' fun-lovin' crowd
Their heart is in the music
And they love to play it loud
There's no forms or no applications
There's no red tape administrations
It's the American Honky-Tonk Bar Association

We're all one big family
Throughout the cities and the towns
We don't reach for handouts
We reach for those who are down
And every local chapter has a seven day a week
Available consultation
For your frustration
It's called an American Honky-Tonk Bar Association

(Repeat Chorus)

ONE NIGHT A DAY
(Gary Burr, Pete Wasner)

There's not a lot of things to do
I wouldn't rather do with you
Guess I'm funny that way

Lately I just sit and stare
I talk to people who aren't there
To get through one night a day

(Chorus)
One night a day
One step away
From leavin' you behind

I sit up with the radio
Sing along with the ones I know
To get through one night a day

(Repeat Chorus)

I'm callin' every friend I've had
Wake 'em up, and make 'em mad

Let 'em know that I'm OK
I used to sit and talk to you
They're all just a substitute
To get through one night a day

(Repeat Chorus)

I stay up with the late, late show
Just another way I know
To get through one night a day
To get through one night a day

KICKIN' AND SCREAMIN'
(Tony Arata)

Well, I don't know what my uncle did
But he must have done it right
They sure strung him up one Saturday night
He had spent his whole life fussin'
Would have spent his last breath cussin'
'Til he realized the deal was really done
He started screamin' "hallelujah"
Tryin' to make his peace with everyone

(Chorus)
Yeah, he was kickin' and screamin'
Just like he came in
He was kickin' and screamin', darlin'
Right to the bitter end
Ain't it funny how we come in kickin' giddyup
And go out hollerin' whoa
Lord, we never want to be here
Sure don't ever want to go

Well, I could hear those church bells ringin'
To my best friend I was clingin'
Screamin' "If you love me brother don't let me go"

Well, then the whole scene was repeated
Two years later I begged and pleaded
Screamin' "If you love me, honey,
Now you know you wouldn't want to let me go"
No, I didn't want to do it
But I sure don't want to see it come undone

(Repeat Chorus Twice)

ANONYMOUS
(Tony Arata, Jon Schwabe)

Well I wrote our names a thousand times
Just to see yours sitting next to mine
Sent you flowers cards unsigned . . . anonymous

In days to come like days that passed
My heart beats for you, always has
Though you know me only as . . . anonymous

In dreams at night I carry your books for you
And when I rise a flame for you
Always too shy to carry the whole thing through

Like the light from that eternal flame
Burns for one without a name
My love forever will remain . . . anonymous

Oh you'll always wonder who it was
Who it was
It was just . . . anonymous

Well I wrote our names a thousand times
Just to see yours sitting next to mine
And I sent you flowers card unsigned

Harmony: Allen Reynolds, Garth Brooks

AIN'T GOING DOWN ('TIL THE SUN COMES UP)

(Kent Blazy, Kim Williams, Garth Brooks)

Six o'clock on Friday evening
Mama doesn't know she's leaving
'Til she hears the screen door slamming
Rubber squealin', gears a-jamming
Local country station
Just a-blarin' on the radio
Pick him up at seven and they're headin' to the rodeo
Mama's on the front porch screamin' out her warning
Girl you'd better get your red head
Back in bed before the morning

Nine o'clock the show is ending
But the fun is just beginning
She knows he's anticipating
But she's gonna keep him waiting
Grab a bite to eat
And then they're headin' to the honky tonk
But loud crowds and line dancing
Just ain't what they really want
Drive out to the boondocks and park down by the creek
And where it's George Strait 'til real late
And dancing cheek to cheek

(Chorus)
Ain't going down 'til the sun comes up
Ain't givin' in 'til they get enough
Going 'round the world in a pickup truck
Ain't goin' down 'til the sun comes up

Ten 'til twelve is wine and dancing
Midnight starts the hard romancing
One o'clock that truck is rocking
Two is comin' still no stopping
Break to check the clock at three
They're right on where they wanna be
And four o'clock get up get going
Five o'clock that rooster's crowing

(Repeat Chorus)

Six o'clock on Saturday
Her folks don't know he's on his way
The stalls are clean the horses fed
They say she's grounded 'til she's dead
And here he comes around the bend
Slowing down she's jumping in
Hey mom your daughter's gone
And there they go again

(Repeat Chorus)

Harmony: Trisha Yearwood, Garth Brooks

THE RED STROKES

(James Garver, Lisa Sanderson, Jenny Yates, Garth Brooks)

Moonlight on canvas, midnight and wine
Two shadows starting to softly combine
The picture they're painting
Is one of the heart
And to those who have seen it
It's a true work of art

(Chorus)
Oh, the red strokes
Passions uncaged
Thundering moments of tenderness rage
Oh, the red strokes
Tempered and strong (Fearlessly drawn)
Burning the night like the dawn

Steam on the window, salt in a kiss
Two hearts have never pounded like this
Inspired by a vision
That they can't command
Erasing the borders
With each brush of a hand

(Repeat Chorus)

Oh, the blues will be blue and the jealousies green
But when love picks its shade it demands to be seen

(Repeat Chorus Twice)

Steam on the window, salt in a kiss
Two hearts have never pounded like this

Harmony: Helen Darling, Garth Brooks

CALLIN' BATON ROUGE
(Dennis Linde)

I spent last night in the arms
Of a girl in Louisiana
And though I'm out on the highway
My thoughts are still with her
Such a strange combination of a woman and a child
Such a strange situation stoppin' every hundred miles
Callin' Baton Rouge

A replay of last night's events
Roll through my mind
Except a scene or two
Erased by sweet red wine
And I see a truck stop sign ahead
So I change lanes
I need a cup of coffee
And a couple dollars change
Callin' Baton Rouge

(Chorus)
Operator won't you put me on through
I gotta' send my love down to Baton Rouge
Hurry up won't you put her on the line
I gotta' talk to the girl just one more time

Hello Samantha dear, I hope you're feelin' fine
And it won't be long until I'm with you all the time
But until then I'll spend my money up
Right down to my last dime
Callin' Baton Rouge

(Repeat Chorus)

Harmony: John Cowan, Sam Bush

THE NIGHT WILL ONLY KNOW
(Stephanie Davis, Jenny Yates, Garth Brooks)

That night will live forever
Their first time to lie together
They were finally where desire dared them to go
Both belonging to another
But longing to be lovers
Promising each other that the night will only know

Parked on some old backstreet
They laid down in the back seat
And fell into the fire down below
But they would pay for their deceiving
For a deadly web was weaving
Why they picked that spot that evening
Lord, the night will only know

(Chorus)
Well within the innuendoes
Just outside the steamy windows
The night was shattered by a woman's scream
Motionless and frightened
The grip of fate had tightened
And with trembling hands they wiped away the steam

They saw a woman pleading
Stumbling, begging and retreating
'Til she became the victim of her foe
And they watched her fall in silence
To save their own alliance
But the reason for the violence
Just the night will only know

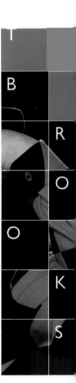

And every paper ran the story
She was stripped of all her glory
And they told exactly how the woman died
Abandoned and forsaken
Too many pills were taken
And they ruled the woman's death a suicide

Bound by their behavior
They could have been her savior
Now guilt becomes the endless debt they owe
But another crime was committed
And it's never been admitted
Have the guilty been acquitted
Lord, the night will only know

Harmony: Kathy Chiavola, Garth Brooks

THE COWBOY SONG

(Roy Robinson)

Pushin' horns weren't easy like the movie said it was
And I don't recall no dance hall girls
Or hotel rooms with rugs
You worked hot and tired and nasty
Rode your pony's head too low
There were all the nights you couldn't sleep
'Cause it was too damn cold
And you'd sing "Strawberry Roan" and "Little Joe"

Like the time we hit the river
And the rains began to fall
And the water was risin' so damn fast
We thought it'd drown us all
We lost a lot of steers that day
And four or five good mounts
But when all the boys rode into camp
We knew that's what counts
And we sang, yippee ti yi yay and "Amazing Grace"

Or the night they broke behind us
And then took us by surprise
I whistled out to Bonner, I seen the terror in his eyes
And he rode for all his horse would ride
And I know he done his best
But he crossed over Jordan ridin' Dunny to his death
And we sang "Bringing In The Sheaves" and "The Rugged Cross"

So when you see the cowboy, he's not ragged by his choice
He never meant to bow them legs
Or put that gravel in his voice
He's just chasin' what he really loves
And what's burnin' in his soul
Wishin' to God that he'd been born a hundred years ago
Still singin' "Strawberry Roan" and "Little Joe"

Harmony: Garth Brooks

THE OLD STUFF

COWBOYS AND ANGELS

THE FEVER

THAT OL' WIND

ROLLIN'

THE CHANGE

THE BEACHES OF CHEYENNE

TO MAKE YOU FEEL MY LOVE

IT'S MIDNIGHT CINDERELLA

SHE'S EVERY WOMAN

IRELAND

FRESH

This album is lovingly dedicated to Bill Boyd. You were a great help to me in the music business and even better, a dear friend. Your family misses you, hoss, so do we.

This album is also dedicated to Oklahoma. My pride and respect for what you went through and how you handled it cannot be measured. And to the world— thanks for helping out a neighbor. My love and thanks to the: Brookses, Smittles, Mahls, and Holdens

H O R S E S

THE OLD STUFF
(Bryan Kennedy, Dan Roberts, Garth Brooks)

Oh I said a little prayer tonight
Before I came on stage
As I came walkin' past the drivers
And the locals on the union wage
I asked the good Lord up in heaven
Let me treat the music right
Then I prayed that Detroit
Goes wild tonight

Seven pickers and all our gear in a rental van
Playin' music never sleepin' and workin' on a neon tan
We played The Barn down in Sanford Florida
For Bev Roberts out in Camden Park
We plugged it in up east at Bull Run
And the place went dark

(Chorus)
Back when the old stuff was new
Back before the buses and the
Hard workin' boys in the crew
It was one big party
But the business called it payin' our dues
Back when the old stuff was new

Oh the stories we could tell
If it weren't for the code of the road
About The Buckboard, Bear Creek, Cowboys, and the Grizzly Rose
You know the weather turned bad in Scottsdale
A tornado nearly stole the show
We just danced in the rain and listened to the thunder roll

Back when the old stuff was new
Hats off to the K.C. Opry and ellA GURU's
It was one big party
Uncle Joe you know we owe it to you
Back when the old stuff was new

No rules young fools comin' from the old school
Takin' on the world alone
Next date can't wait tearin' up the interstate
Every place we played was home
Balls out no doubt this is what it's all about
Beggin' for a place to play
Swingin' with our low friends
Prayin' that it never ends
Wouldn't trade a single day

(Repeat Chorus)

Hey it's still one big party
You can call it whatever you choose
You make me feel like the old stuff is new

Harmonies: Trisha Yearwood and Garth Brooks

COWBOYS AND ANGELS
(Kent Blazy, Kim Williams, Garth Brooks)

On the eighth day God noticed a problem
For there below Him stood a cowboy alone
Stubborn and proud, reckless and loud
God knew he'd never make it on his own
So God looked out all over creation
And listened as that cowboy prayed
God took passion and thunder
Patience and wonder then He sent down
The best thing that God ever made

Cowboys and angels leather and lace
Salt of the earth meets heavenly grace
Cowboys and angels tested and tried
It's a long way to heaven
And one hell of a ride

Nothin's changed since the dawn of creation
For you will find them together today
And only heaven above them knows why she loves him
But he must be the reason she don't fly away

Cowboys and angels leather and lace
Salt of the earth meets heavenly grace
Cowboys and angels tested and tried
It's a long way to heaven
And one hell of a ride

It's a long way to heaven
And one hell of a ride

Harmonies: Trisha Yearwood and Garth Brooks

THE FEVER
(Steven Tyler, Joe Perry, Bryan Kennedy, Dan Roberts)

He's got a split finger wrap
And his rope's pulled way too tight
He's got a lunatic smile
'Cause he's really drawn deep tonight

He's got a fever, fever, fever, fever
Grab a hold of anything and hold on tight
It hits you like the venom from a rattlesnake bite
We're all here 'cause he's not all there tonight

He takes one last breath
And time turns inside out
Then the gate busts open
To the world he dreams about

He's got a fever, fever, fever, fever
Stick a rope on anything 'cause he don't care
He'd even take a ride in an electric chair
We're all here 'cause he's not all there tonight

He says it's really kinda simple
Keep your mind in the middle
While your butt spins 'round and 'round
Take heed to Sankey's preachin'
Keep liftin' and reachin'
And ridin' like there ain't no clowns

What he loves might kill him
But he's got no choice
He's a different breed
With a voice down deep inside
That's screamin' he was born to ride

He's got a fever, fever, fever, fever
Fever makes you crazy 'cause it makes no sense
Like runnin' from your shadow out of self-defense
But he won't run and baby he can't hide
He thinks the odds are even leavin' one hand tied
He gets so tired of hangin' on so tight
I know you think he's crazy well I think you're right
We're all here 'cause he's not all there that's right

Harmonies: Garth Brooks

THAT OL' WIND

(Leigh Reynolds, Garth Brooks)

She dropped her boy at school on time
One less worry on her mind
Now it's off to work and on the radio
Comes an old familiar song
And then the D.J.'s voice comes on
And says he's back in town tonight for one last show

Her eyes well up with tears
God could it be it's been ten years
Since that Autumn night outside the county fair
When two strangers shared a night
And in the darkness found a light
That to this day is still alive and burning there

He asked her twice to come along
They said good-bye at the break of dawn
'Cause you can't hold back the wind
If it's meant to be again
Then someday he'll find his way back to her arms

The marquee misspelled his name
And not too many people came
But that didn't matter to them
They laughed and loved all through the night
And as they faced the morning light
They found themselves standing there again

And he asked her twice to come along
They said good-bye at the break of dawn
As his bus left out she cried
With him standing by her side
That ol' wind had once again found its way home

Someday he'll tell her about the money he hid
And someday she'll tell him that the boy is his kid
But for right now they're both in love
The only thing they're thinkin' of
Is that they're finally where their hearts have always been

ROLLIN'

(Harley Allen, Leigh Reynolds, Garth Brooks)

She was born to a mother trucker
Raised behind the wheel
So you can blame it on the highway
For the way she can't sit still
She says life is like a windshield
It ain't no rear view mirror
The only way to get where you're goin'
Is find that higher gear
And keep it

Rollin'
Life's gonna run you over if you don't get goin'
She said I wanna feel the earth move under me
Movin' with the motion of a melody
Oh I get the blues if the rhythm ain't got no soul
You gotta keep it
Rollin'

Well I knew that I was in trouble
When she told me that talk was cheap
Said if you're tired get on the sofa
'Cause the bed's no place to sleep
Then she reached out and she kissed me
Lord it knocked me to my knees
And I knew if I was gonna get naked
I was gonna have to roll up my sleeves
And keep it

Rollin'
Love was gonna run me over if I didn't get goin'
She said I wanna feel the earth move under me
Movin' with the motion of a melody
Boy I get the blues if the rhythm ain't got no soul
You got to keep it
Rollin'

So I talked her into gettin' married
But she wouldn't hang up her wheels
I was afraid I'd take a back seat
To the way the highway feels
But each day she's pullin' over
More than she used to
She knows love is like the highway
The main thing you gotta do
Is keep it rollin'

Accidental Harmonies: Trisha Yearwood and Garth Brooks

THE CHANGE
(Tony Arata, Wayne Tester)

One hand
Reaches out
And pulls a lost soul from harm
While a thousand more
Go unspoken for
They say what good have you done
By saving just this one
It's like whispering a prayer
In the fury of a storm

And I hear them saying you'll never change things
And no matter what you do it's still the same thing
But it's not the world that I am changing
I do this so this world will know
That it will not change me

This heart
Still believes
That love and mercy still exist
While all the hatreds rage and so many say
That love is all but pointless in madness such as this
It's like trying to stop a fire
With the moisture from a kiss
And I hear them saying you'll never change things
And no matter what you do it's still the same thing
But it's not the world that I am changing
I do this so this world will know
That it will not change me

As long as one heart still holds on
Then hope is never really gone

I hear them saying you'll never change things
And no matter what you do it's still the same thing
But it's not the world that I am changing
I do this so this world we know
Never changes me

What I do is so
This world will know
That it will not change me

THE BEACHES OF CHEYENNE
(Dan Roberts, Bryan Kennedy, Garth Brooks)

They packed up all his buckles
And shipped his saddle to his dad
And by the way the house looked
She must have took it bad
The workers come on Monday
To fix the door and patch the wall
They say she just went crazy
The night she got the call

He was up in Wyoming
And drew a bull no man could ride
He promised her he'd turn out
Well it turned out that he lied
And their dreams that they'd been livin'
In the California sand
Died right there beside him
In Cheyenne

They say she just went crazy
Screamin' out his name
She ran out into the ocean
And to this day they claim
That if you go down by the water
You'll see her footprints in the sand
'Cause every night she walks the beaches of Cheyenne

They never found her body
Just her diary by the bed
It told about the fight they had
And the words that she had said
When he told her he was ridin'
She said then I don't give a damn
If you never come back from Cheyenne

They say she just went crazy
Screamin' out his name
She ran out into the ocean
And to this day they claim
That you can go down by the water
And see her footprints in the sand
'Cause every night she walks the beaches of Cheyenne

Nobody can explain it
Some say she's still alive
They even claim they've seen her
On the shoreline late at night
So if you go down by the water
You'll see her footprints in the sand
'Cause every night she walks the beaches of Cheyenne

Every night she walks the beaches of Cheyenne

Harmonies: Trisha Yearwood and Garth Brooks

TO MAKE YOU FEEL MY LOVE
(Bob Dylan)

When the rain is blowing in your face
And the whole world is on your case
I could offer you a warm embrace
To make you feel my love

When evening shadows and the stars appear
And there is no one to dry your tears
I could hold you for a million years
To make you feel my love

I know you haven't made your mind up yet
But I would never do you wrong
I've known it from the moment that we met
There's no doubt in my mind where you belong

I'd go hungry, I'd go black and blue
I'd go crawling down the avenue
There ain't nothing' that I wouldn't do
To make you feel my love

The storms are raging on a rolling sea
And on the highway of regret
The winds of change are blowing wild and free
You ain't see nothin' like me yet

There ain't nothin' that I wouldn't do
Go to the ends of the earth for you
Make you happy make your dreams come true
To make you feel my love

Harmony: Garth Brooks

IT'S MIDNIGHT CINDERELLA
(Kim Williams, Kent Blazy, Garth Brooks)

It's midnight Cinderella but don't you worry none
'Cause I'm Peter Peter the Pumpkin Eater
And the party's just begun

I guess your prince charming
Wasn't after all

'Cause he sure seemed different
Right after the ball
I guess more than horses
Are turnin' into rats
And by the way he's walkin'
I can guess where your slipper's at

(Chorus)
It's midnight Cinderella time that you should know
There's gonna be some changes in the way this story goes
It's midnight Cinderella but don't you worry none
'Cause I'm Peter Peter the Pumpkin Eater
And the party's just begun

I'm gonna help you get over
Bein' under that spell
You're gonna learn to love midnight
Inside this pumpkin shell
I gotta few new magic tricks
Your godmother can't do
I'll show you what it means to
Bip, bip, bip, bip, boppity boo

(Repeat Chorus)

I'm Peter Peter the Pumpkin Eater
And the party has now begun

Harmonies: Trisha Yearwood and Garth Brooks

SHE'S EVERY WOMAN
(Victoria Shaw, Garth Brooks)

She's sun and rain, she's fire and ice
A little crazy but it's nice
And when she gets mad, you best leave her alone
'Cause she'll rage just like a river
Then she'll beg you to forgive her
She's every woman that I've ever known

She's so New York and then L.A.
And every town along the way
She's every place that I've never been
She's making love on rainy nights
She's a stroll through Christmas lights
And she's everything I want to do again

It needs no explanation
'Cause it all makes perfect sense
For when it comes down to temptation
She's on both sides of the fence

No it needs no explanation
'Cause it all makes perfect sense
When it comes down to temptation
She's on both sides of the fence

She's anything but typical
She's so unpredictable
Oh but even at her worst she ain't that bad
She's as real as real can be
And she's every fantasy
Lord she's every lover that I've ever had
And she's every lover that I've never had

Harmonies: Susan Ashton and Garth Brooks

IRELAND
(Stephanie Davis, Jenny Yates, Garth Brooks)

They say mother earth is breathing
With each wave that finds the shore
Her soul rises in the evening
For to open twilight's door
Her eyes are the stars in heaven
Watching o'er us all the while
And her heart it is in Ireland
Deep within the Emerald Isle

We are forty against hundreds
In someone else's bloody war
We know not why we're fighting
Or what we're dying for
They will storm us in the morning
When the sunlight turns the sky
Death is waiting for its dance now
Fate has sentenced us to die

(Chorus)
Ireland I am coming home
I can see your rolling fields of green
And fences made of stone
I am reaching out won't you take my hand
I'm coming home Ireland

Oh the captain he lay bleeding
I can hear him calling me
These men are yours now for the leading
Show them to their destiny
And as I look up all around me
I see the ragged tired and torn
I tell them to make ready
'Cause we're not waiting for the morn

(Repeat Chorus)

Now the fog is deep and heavy
As we forge the dark and fear
We can hear their horses breathing
As in silence we draw near
There are no words to be spoken
Just a look to say good-bye
I draw a breath and night is broken
As I scream our battle cry

(Repeat Chorus)

I am home Ireland

garth brooks

Alabama Clay 66

Cowboy Bill 70

The Dance 73

Everytime That It Rains 76

I Know One 79

If Tomorrow Never Comes 84

I've Got A Good Thing Going 82

Much Too Young (To Feel This Damn Old) . . .90

Nobody Gets Off In This Town 94

Not Counting You .87

Uptown Down-Home Good Ol' Boy 98

ALABAMA CLAY

Words and Music by
LARRY CORDLE and RONNY SCAIFE

Alabama Clay - 4 - 1

68

Verse 2:
Now the city's just a prison without fences;
His job is just a routine he can't stand.
And at night he dreams of wide-open spaces,
Fresh dirt between his toes and on his hands.
Then one day a picture came inside a letter,
Of a young girl with a baby in her arms.
And the words she wrote would change his life forever,
So he went to raise his family on the farm.
(To Chorus 2:)

COWBOY BILL

Words and Music by
LARRY BASTIAN and ED BERGHOFF

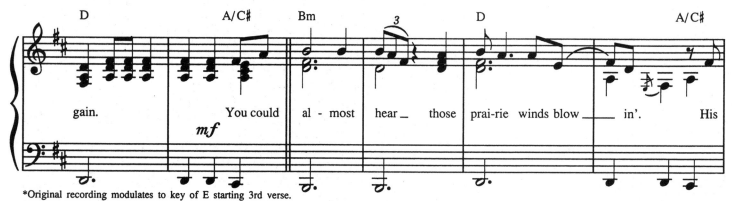

*Original recording modulates to key of E starting 3rd verse.

Cowboy Bill - 3 - 1

sad-dle ____ a creak-in', 'neath his old ____ fad-ed jeans. ____ You could taste ____

____ the dry dust ____ from the trail ____ he was rid-in', as he sat there and he paint-

-ed those west Tex-as scenes. ____ {1. 2. And the / 3. And the} {grown-ups would tell ____ us ____ / grown-ups that told ____ us ____} "You

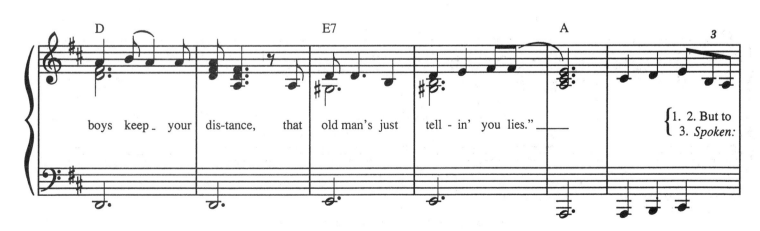

boys keep ____ your dis-tance, that old man's just tell-in' you lies." ____ {1. 2. But to / 3. *Spoken:*}

Verse 2:
He told us of a time when he rode with the rangers,
Down on the Pecos and he saved the day.
Outnumbered by plenty, they were almost to cover,
With thirty banditos headed their way.
He looked back just in time to see a horse stumble,
The captain went down and Bill pulled up on his reins.
And through a flurry a bullets he rescued the captain,
They rode for a sunset, just the story remains.
(To Chorus:)

Verse 3:
I still remember the day that it happened,
We waited and waited but Bill never showed.
And the folks at the feed store said they hadn't seen him,
So we set out his place down the old Grist Mill Road.
And we cried when we found him lying there with his mem'ries,
The old trunk wide open, things scattered about.
He was clutchin' a badge that said "Texas Ranger",
And an old "Yeller" letter said Texas is proud.
(To Chorus:)

THE DANCE

Words and Music by
TONY ARATA

The Dance - 3 - 1

EVERYTIME THAT IT RAINS

Words and Music by
CHARLEY STEFL, TY ENGLAND
and GARTH BROOKS

*Original recording modulates to
key of E♭ starting on 3rd verse.

Everytime That It Rains - 3 - 1

Verse 2:
I played "Please come to Boston" on the jukebox
She said "Hey, that's my favorite song."
The next thing I knew, the song was long through,
And we were still dancin' along.
And with that look in her eye, she pulled from me,
Then she pulled off that apron she wore.
And with her hand in mine, we turned off the sign,
And locked the rain outside the door.
(To Chorus:)

Verse 3:
One late rainy night I got a phone call,
So I went back to see her again.
And through the dance we both stumbled,
And with the buttons we fumbled,
So we decided to call it at friends.
If we ever had a thing now it's over,
And only the memory remains;
Of a roadside cafe on a September day,
I relive every time that it rains.
(To Chorus:)

I KNOW ONE

Words and Music by
JACK CLEMENT

I Know One - 3 - 1

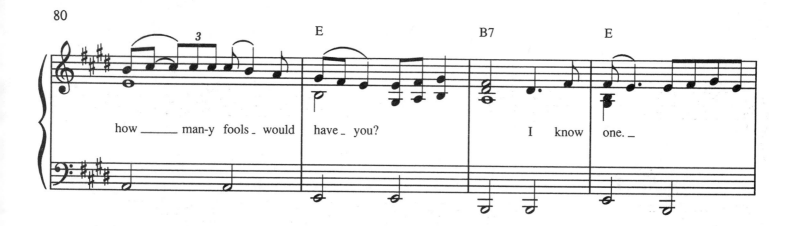

how _____ man-y fools _ would have _ you? I know one. _

Bridge:

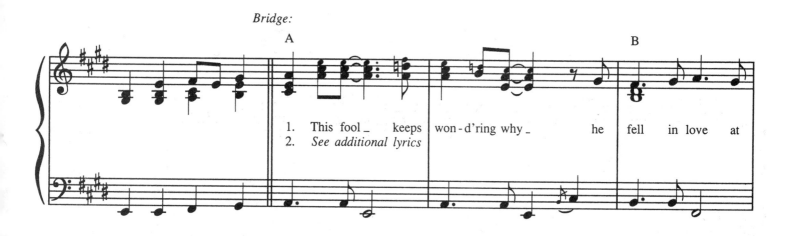

1. This fool _ keeps won-d'ring why _ he fell in love at
2. *See additional lyrics*

all. _ But you might need this fool _____ a - round in case _ you

Chorus:

fall.

1. Af-ter the par - ty's o - ver, _ and
2. Af-ter your heart's been bro-ken, _ and

mf

you've had your fill of fun, if you need a fool to for - give _ you, _
you need a place to run, if you'll take a fool who _ loves _ you, _

I know one. _
I know

one. _

Mm _____

_____

I know one. _

Bridge 2:
You never know you might be lonely when all your loves have missed.
It wouldn't hurt to keep an extra fool on your list.
(To Chorus:)

I'VE GOT A GOOD THING GOING

Words and Music by
LARRY BASTIAN, SANDY MAHL
and GARTH BROOKS

I've Got a Good Thing Going - 2 - 1

Verse 2:
By now she must be tired of always giving,
And tired of what she's getting in return.
I guess Oklahoma's more her style of living,
'Cause I can see her heart is heading,
'Cross a bridge I thought she's burned.
(To Chorus:)

IF TOMORROW NEVER COMES

Words and Music by
KENT BLAZY and GARTH BROOKS

If Tomorrow Never Comes - 3 - 1

Verse 2:
'Cause I've lost loved ones in my life.
Who never knew how much I loved them.
Now I live with the regret
That my true feelings for them never were revealed.
So I made a promise to myself
To say each day how much she means to me
And avoid that circumstance
Where there's no second chance to tell her how I feel. ('Cause)
(To Chorus:)

NOT COUNTING YOU

Words and Music by
GARTH BROOKS

Not Counting You - 3 - 1

I've ne-ver lost __ at love __ not count-ing you. __

1. *To Next Strain* 2. *D.S.S.* 3.

Chorus:

Not count-ing you, __

(end solo)

3. I've

Not count-ing you, __

I've

Instrumental solo 3rd time

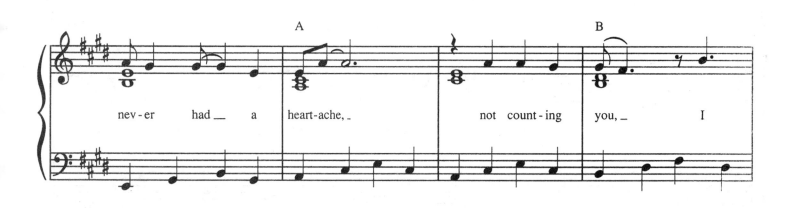

nev-er had __ a heart-ache, __ not count-ing you, __ I

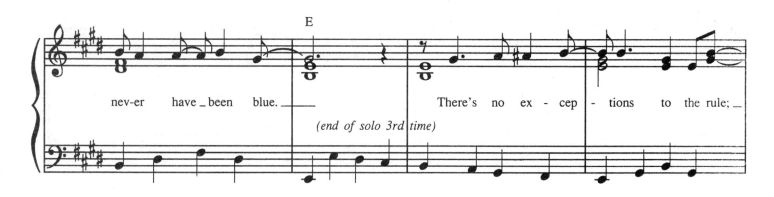

nev-er have __ been blue. __

(end of solo 3rd time)

There's no ex - cep - tions to the rule; __

Verse 2:
I've never got down on my knees and asked the Lord above,
If He would only bring to me the one I'm dreaming of.
Begging to be taken back and swearing I'll be true,
Has never crossed my mind not counting you.
(To Chorus:)

MUCH TOO YOUNG
(To Feel This Damn Old)

Words and Music by
RANDY TAYLOR and GARTH BROOKS

Freely ♩ = 80

with Pedal

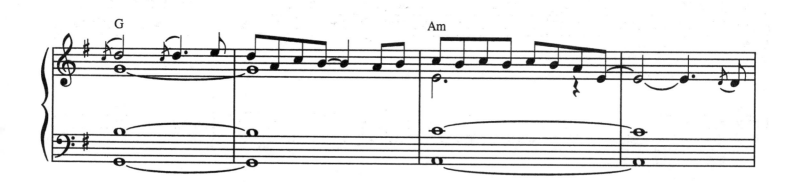

Much Too Young - 4 - 1

Verse: **Country two-beat** ♩ = 80

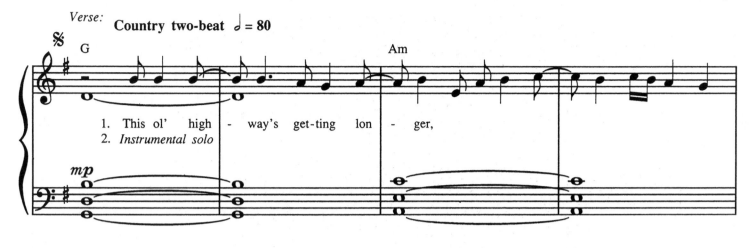

1. This ol' high - way's get-ting lon - ger,
2. *Instrumental solo*

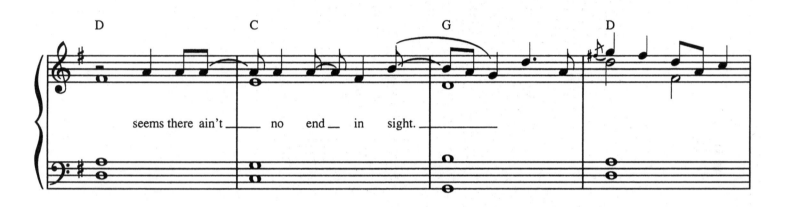

seems there ain't ___ no end ___ in sight. ___

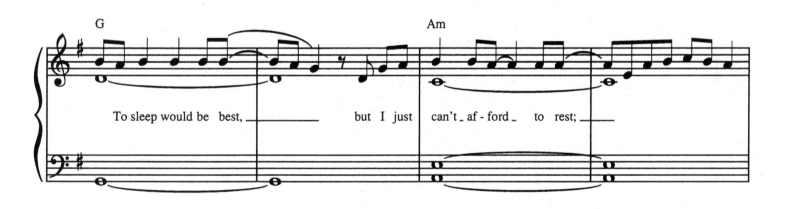

To sleep would be best, ___ but I just can't _ af - ford _ to rest; ___

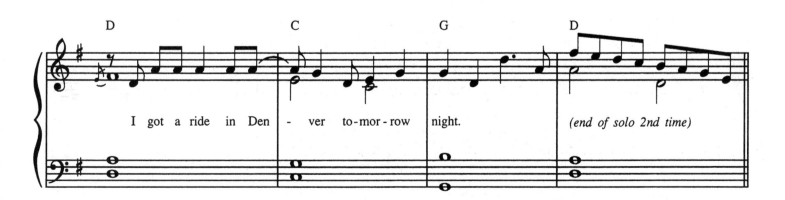

I got a ride in Den - ver to-mor-row night. *(end of solo 2nd time)*

Verse 2:
(Instrumental solo for 16 measures)
The competition's getting younger;
Tougher broncs, you know I can't recall.
A worn out tape of Chris LeDoux, lonely woman and bad booze,
Seem to be the only friends I've left at all.
(To Chorus:)

NOBODY GETS OFF IN THIS TOWN

Words and Music by
LARRY BASTIAN and DEWAYNE BLACKWELL

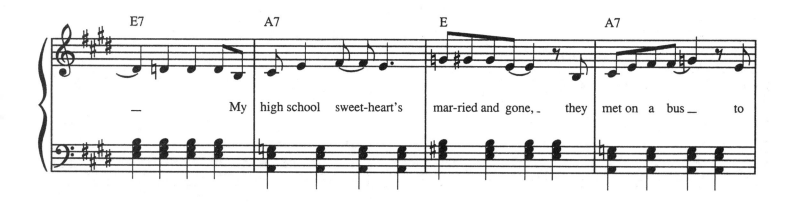

Nobody Gets off in This Town - 4 - 1

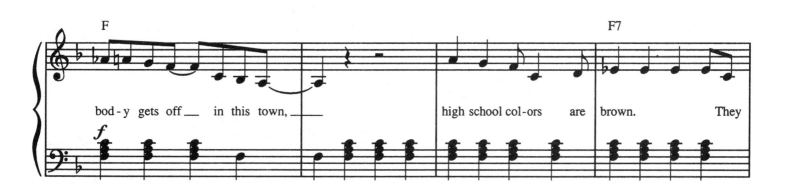

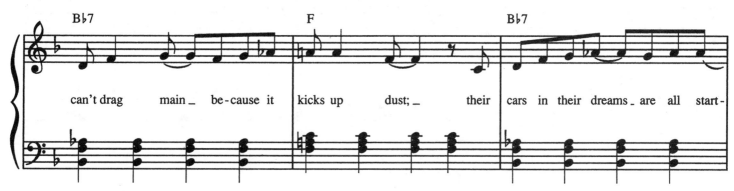

Verse 2:
Nobody gets off in this town,
Folks 'round here wear a frown.
Now let me see if I can set the scene,
It's a one-dog town and he's old and mean.
There's one stop light but it's always green,
Nobody gets off in this town.
(To Verse 3:)

UPTOWN DOWN-HOME GOOD OL' BOY

Words and Music by
DEWAYNE BLACKWELL and
EARL BUD LEE

Moderately fast country ♩ = 144

Uptown Down-home Good Ol' Boy - 4 - 1

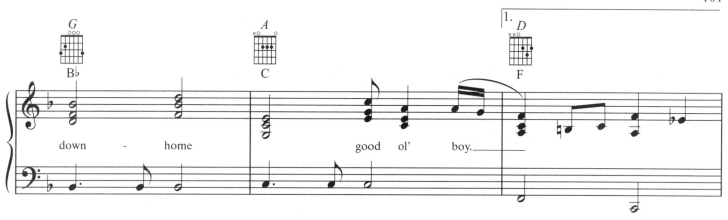

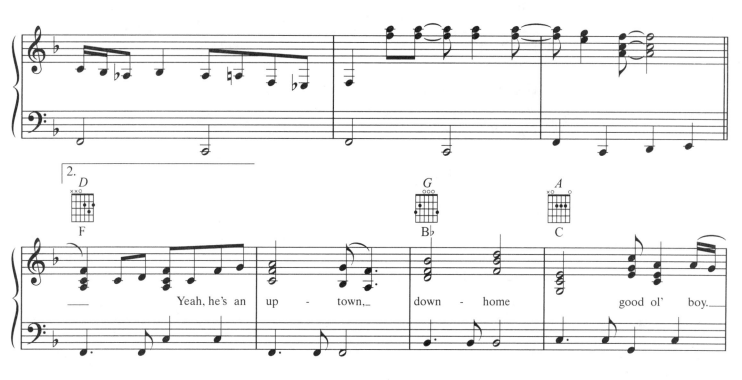

Verse 2:
But you can't keep a good man down.
A line of western wear uptown heard of his fame
And they bought his name.
Now he looks down from a suite
At the silver limo parked out on the street.
And he's not just a face in a martini crowd.
He drinks long-neck Bud and gets a little loud,
And lands back on his feet.
(To Chorus:)

Verse 3:
A woman loved him through it all,
Through his rowdy days and his hardest fall.
When he almost died, she stayed by his side.
She's still right there today.
He wouldn't have it any other way.
And he never did get too proud
To hang out with the same old crowd.
We're proud to say:
(To Chorus:)

Friends In Low Places...............................103

Mr. Blue..106

New Way To Fly.......................................112

Same Old Story 109

This Ain't Tennessee 116

The Thunder Rolls..................................120

Two Of A Kind, Workin' On A Full House........124

Unanswered Prayers...............................127

Victim Of The Game................................132

Wild Horses..138

Wolves 135

NO FENCES

FRIENDS IN LOW PLACES

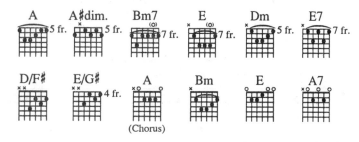

Words and Music by
DEWAYNE BLACKWELL and
EARL BUD LEE

Moderate country rock ♩ = 100

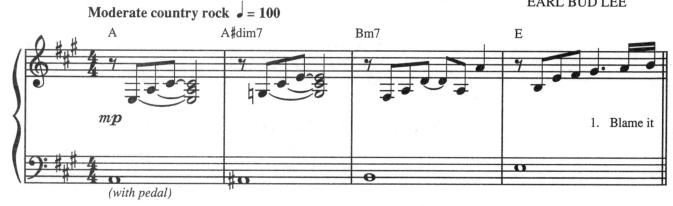

(with pedal)

1. Blame it

Verse:

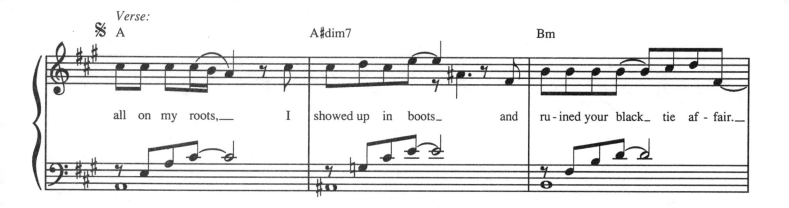

all on my roots,___ I showed up in boots___ and ru-ined your black___ tie af-fair.___

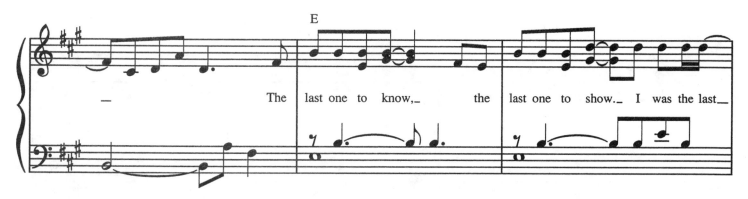

— The last one to know,___ the last one to show.___ I was the last___

Friends in Low Places - 3 - 1

_one you thought you'd see there.___ And I saw the sur - prise,___ and the

A#dim7   Bm7   Dm

fear in his eyes___ when I took his glass__ of cham-pagne.____ And

E7

I toast-ed you,__ said hon - ey, we may be through,__ but you'll nev - er hear__ me com - plain.__

cresc. poco a poco

D/F#   E/G#   *Chorus:* A

_____ 'Cause I've got friends__ in low plac - es where the

f

Verse 2:
Well, I guess I was wrong.
I just don't belong.
But then, I've been there before.
Everything's all right.
I'll just say goodnight,
And I'll show myself to the door.
Hey, I didn't mean
To cause a big scene.
Just give me an hour and then,
Well, I'll be as high
As that ivory tower
That you're livin' in.
(To Chorus:)

MR. BLUE

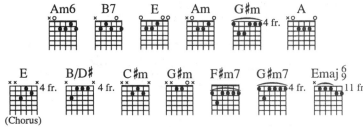

Words and Music by
DEWAYNE BLACKWELL

Mr. Blue - 3 - 1

Verse 2:
I'm Mr. Blue
When you say you're sorry,
Then turn around headed for the lights of town,
Hurtin' me through and through.
Call me Mr. Blue.
(To Bridge:)

Verses 3 & 5:
I won't tell you
When you paint the town
A bright red, to turn it upside down.
I'm painting it too,
But I'm painting it blue.

Verse 4:
(Instrumental solo)
(To Bridge:)

SAME OLD STORY

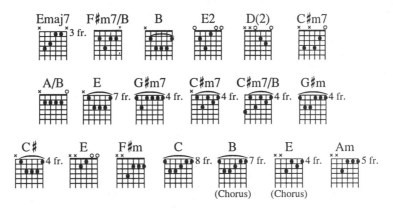

Words and Music by
TONY ARATA

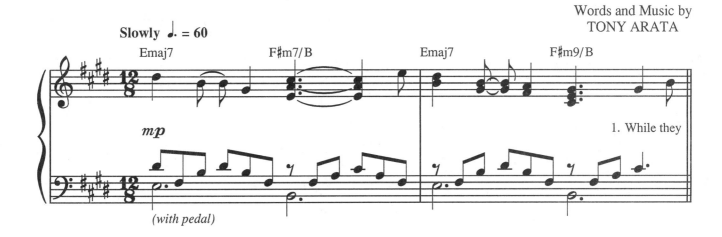

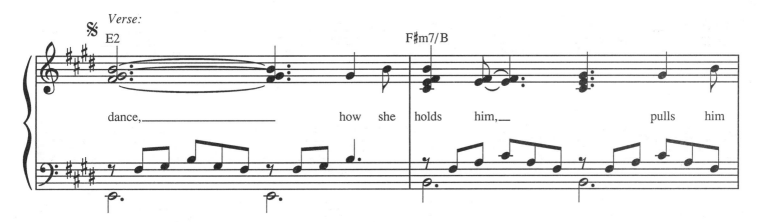

Same Old Story - 3 - 1

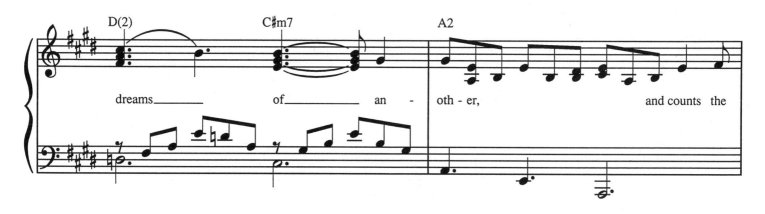

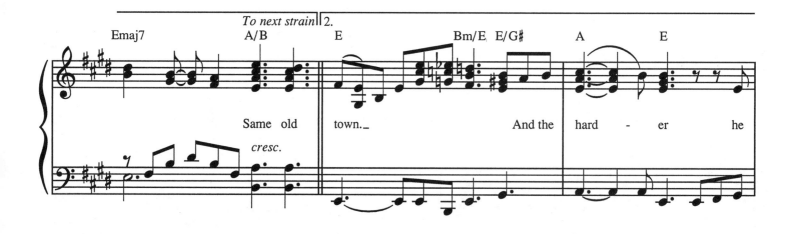

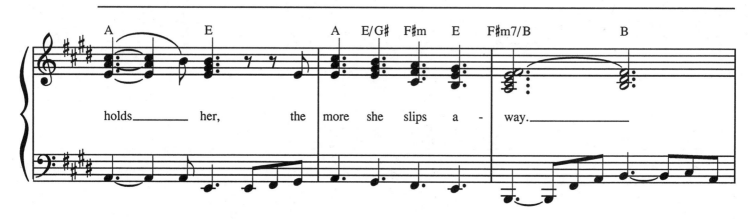

Verse 2:
While they ride,
Lord, he tells her
How they two will settle down.
But she only hears the highway,
And a voice in some other town.
And the harder he holds her,
The more she slips away.
(To Chorus:)

NEW WAY TO FLY

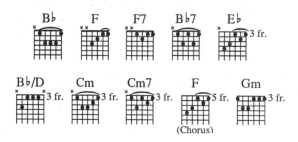

Words and Music by
KIM WILLIAMS
and GARTH BROOKS

1. Like birds on a high line, they line up____ at

night time____ at the bar.____ They all were once

New Way to Fly - 4 - 1

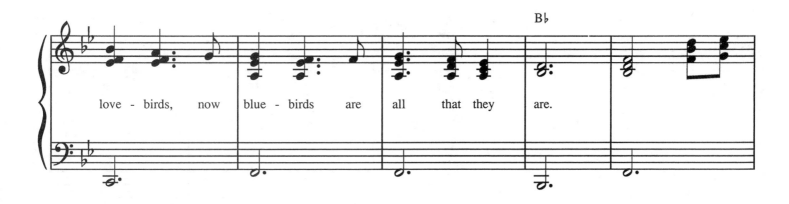

love - birds, now blue - birds are all that they are.

They land - ed in hell___ the min-ute they fell___ from love's

sky.___ And now they hope in___ the wine___ that they'll find a

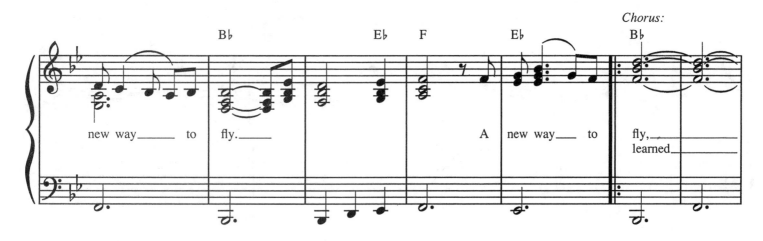

new way___ to fly.___ A new way___ to fly,___
learned___

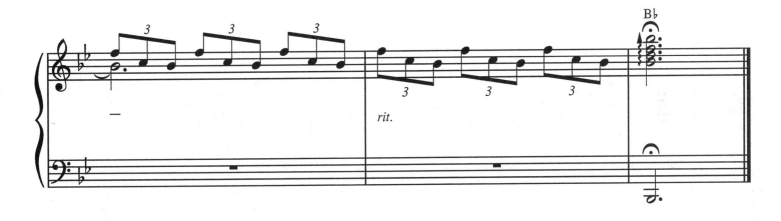

Verse 2:
By the end of the night,
They'll be high as a kite once again.
And they don't seem to mind all the time
Or the money they spend.
It's a high price to pay
To just find a way to get by.
But it's worth every dime
If they find a new way to fly.
(To Chorus:)

THIS AIN'T TENNESSEE

Words and Music by
JAMES SHAW and LARRY BASTIAN

Verse 2:
There'a a bedroom suite
Where she comes to me.
And as her fingers touch my face,
I close my eyes and I fantasize
Another time and place.
What she feels is so warm and real,
And I know her love is true,
And she tries so hard to please,
Still I think sometimes she sees
That this ain't Tennessee
And she ain't you.
(To Bridge:)

THE THUNDER ROLLS

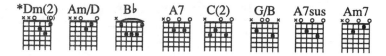

*Alternate between E and F on the 1st string.

Words and Music by
PAT ALGER and
GARTH BROOKS

Slow rock ♩ = 84

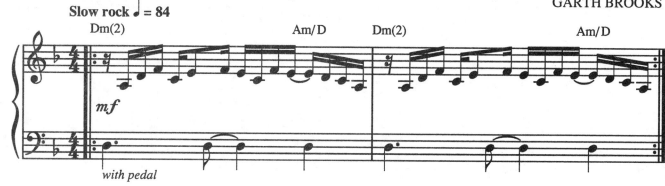

with pedal

Verse:

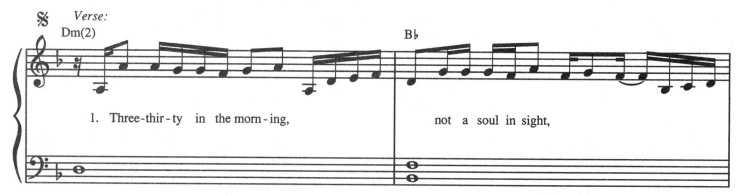

1. Three-thir-ty in the morn-ing,   not a soul in sight,

the cit-y's look-in' like a ghost town   on a   moon-less sum-mer night.___

Rain-drops on the wind-shield,   there's a   storm mov-ing in.___

The Thunder Rolls - 4 - 1

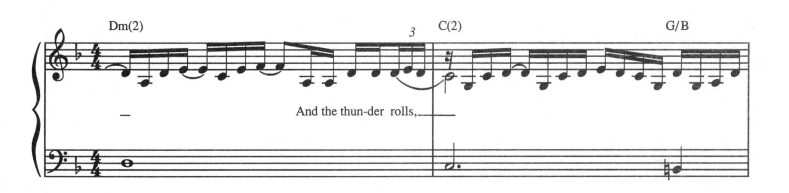

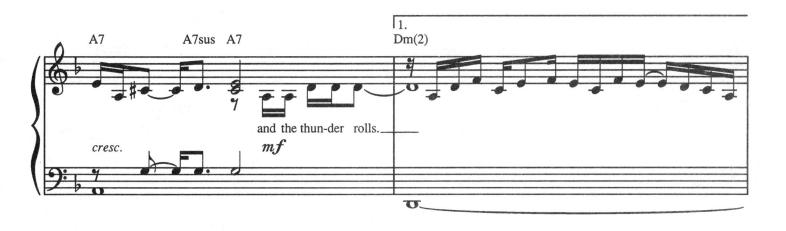

The Thunder Rolls - 4 - 2

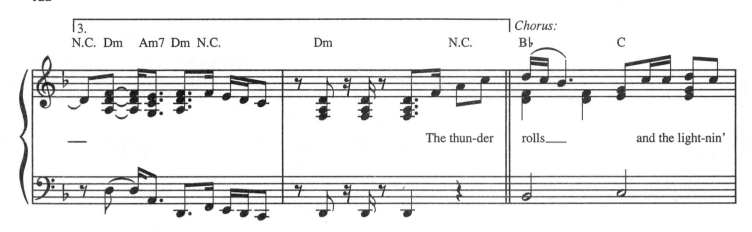

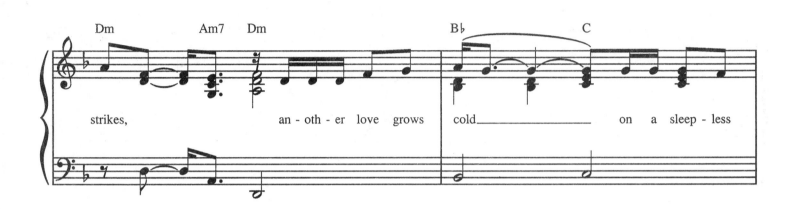

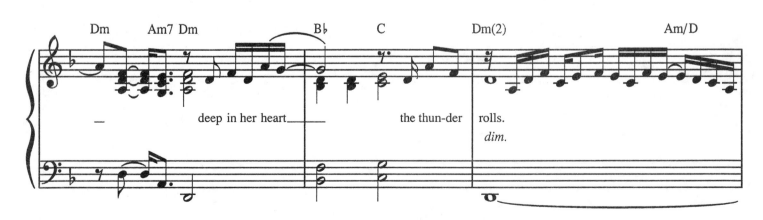

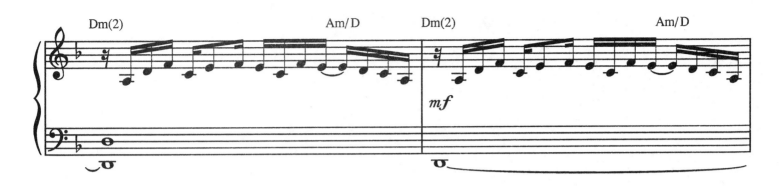

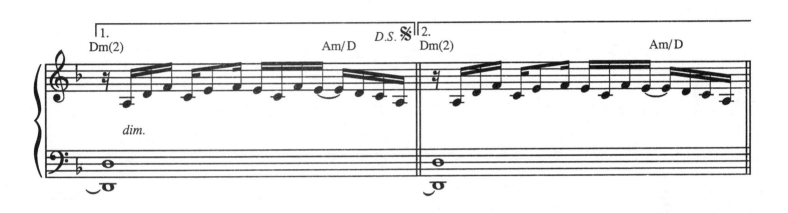

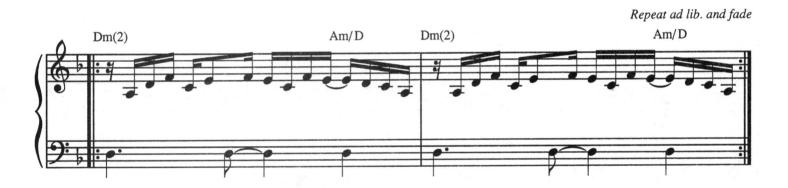

Verse 2:
Every light is burnin'
In a house across town.
She's pacin' by the telephone
In her faded flannel gown,
Askin' for a miracle,
Hopin' she's not right.
Prayin' it's the weather
That's kept him out all night.
And the thunder rolls,
And the thunder rolls.
(To Chorus:)

Verse 3:
She's waitin' by the window
When he pulls into the drive.
She rushes out to hold him,
Thankful he's alive.
But on the wind and rain
A strange new perfume blows,
And the lightnin' flashes in her eyes,
And he knows that she knows.
And the thunder rolls,
And the thunder rolls.
(To Chorus:)

TWO OF A KIND, WORKIN' ON A FULL HOUSE

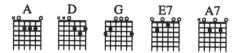

Words and Music by
BOBBY BOYD, WARREN DALE HAYNES
and DENNIS ROBBINS

Two of a Kind, Workin' on a Full House - 3 - 1

To Coda

Yeah, we're two of a kind,___ work - in' on___ a full

house. 2. She wakes___ house. 1. Yeah, a pick -

Bridge:

- up truck___ is her lim - ou - sine.___ And her fa - vor - ite dress is her

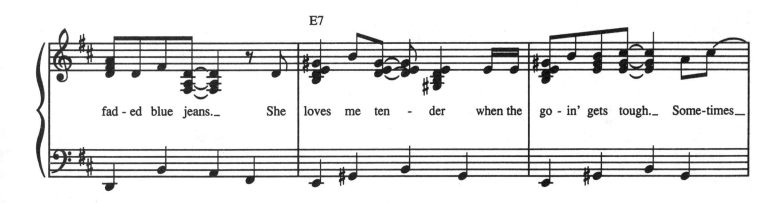

fad - ed blue jeans.___ She loves me ten - der when the go - in' gets tough.___ Some - times___

Two of a Kind, Workin' on a Full House - 3 - 2

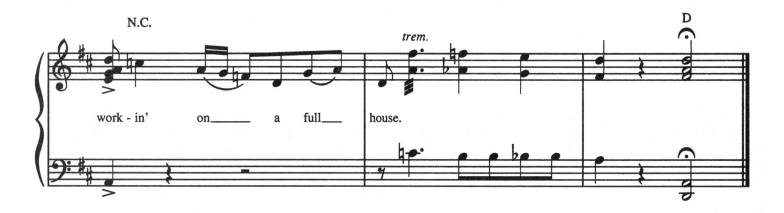

Verse 2:
She wakes me every mornin'
With a smile and a kiss.
Her strong country lovin' is hard to resist.
She's my easy lovin' woman,
I'm her hard-workin' man, no doubt.
Yeah, we're two of a kind
Workin' on a full house. *(To Bridge:)*

Verse 3:
Lord, I need that little woman
Like the crops need rain.
She's my honeycomb, and I'm her sugar cane.
We really fit together
If you know what I'm talkin' about.
Yeah, we're two of a kind
Workin' on a full house. *(To Bridge 2:)*

Bridge 2:
This time I found a keeper, I made up my mind.
Lord, the perfect combination is her heart and mine.
The sky's the limit, no hill is too steep.
We're playin' for fun, but we're playin' for keeps.

Verse 4:
So draw the curtain, honey.
Turn the lights down low.
We'll find some country music on the radio.
I'm yours and you're mine.
Hey, that's what it's all about.
Yeah, we're two of a kind
Workin' on a full house.
Lordy mama, we'll be two of a kind
Workin' on a full house.

UNANSWERED PRAYERS

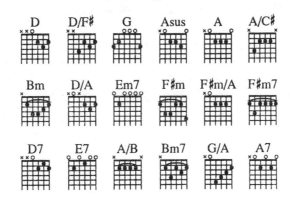

Words and Music by
LARRY B. BASTIAN, PAT ALGER
and GARTH BROOKS

Slowly ♩ = 66

(with pedal)

Verse:

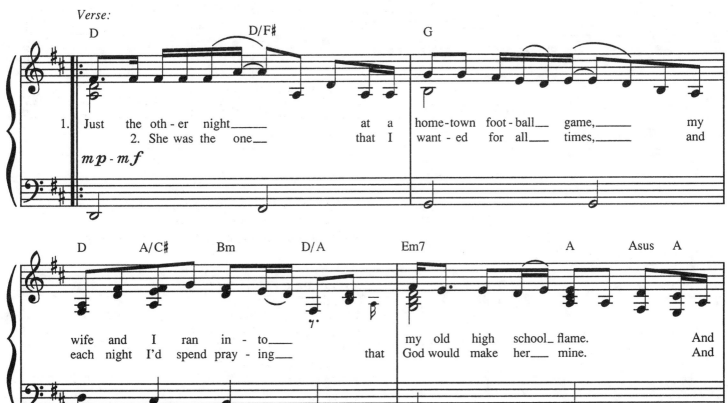

1. Just the oth-er night_____ at a home-town foot-ball_ game,_____ my
2. She was the one_____ that I want-ed for all_ times,_____ and

wife and I ran in-to_____ my old high school_ flame. And
each night I'd spend pray-ing_____ that God would make her_ mine. And

Unanswered Prayers - 5 - 1

as I in - tro - duced_ them_ the past came back to me_____ and I
if He'd on - ly grant_ me____ this wish I'd wished back then_____ I'd

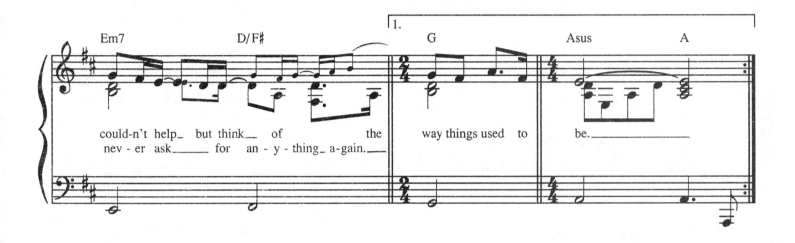

1.

could-n't help_ but think_ of the way things used to be._____
nev - er ask_____ for an - y - thing_ a - gain.___

2.

Chorus:

Some-times I____ thank God_____ for

un - an-swered prayers._ Re - mem-ber when you're talk - in' to the Man up - stairs_ that just be-cause_

He does-n't an - swer does-n't mean He don't care,_____ 'cause some of

To Coda ⊕

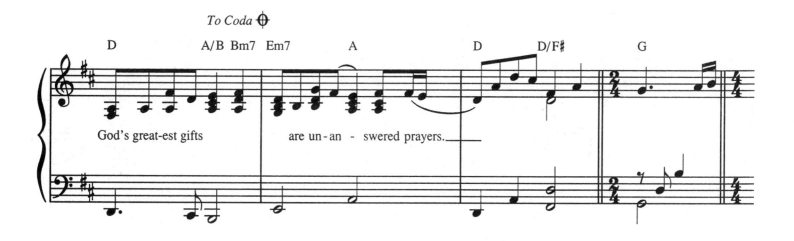

God's great-est gifts are un-an - swered prayers._____

Verse:

3. She was-n't quite the an - gel_____ that I re-

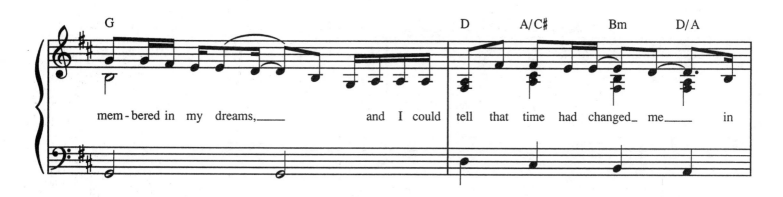

mem-bered in my dreams,_____ and I could tell that time had changed_ me_____ in

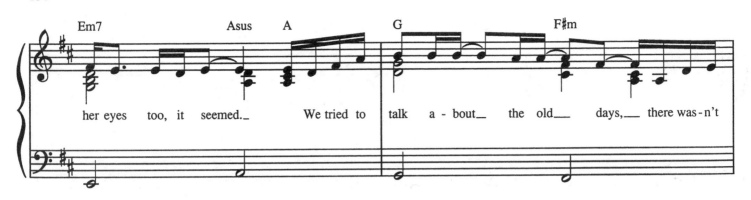

her eyes too, it seemed.___ We tried to talk a-bout___ the old___ days,___ there was-n't

much we could___ re-call.___ I guess the Lord knows what he's do-ing af-ter

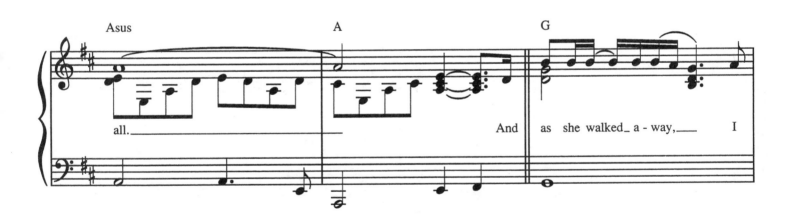

all.___ And as she walked__ a-way,___ I

looked at my wife,_____ and then and there I thanked the good__ Lord for the

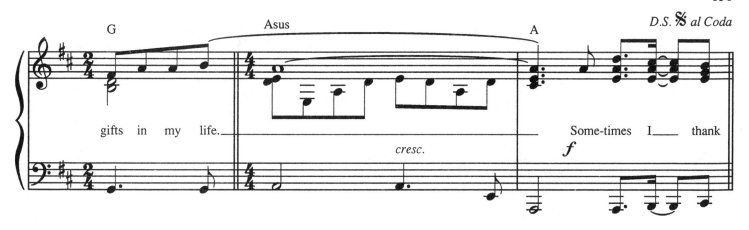

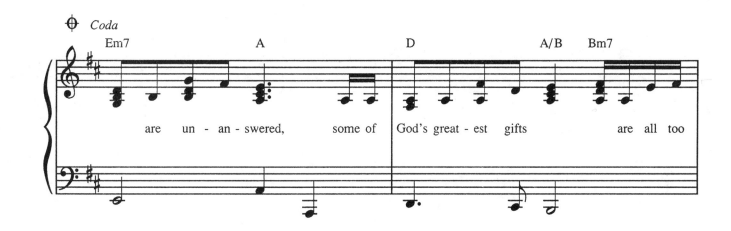

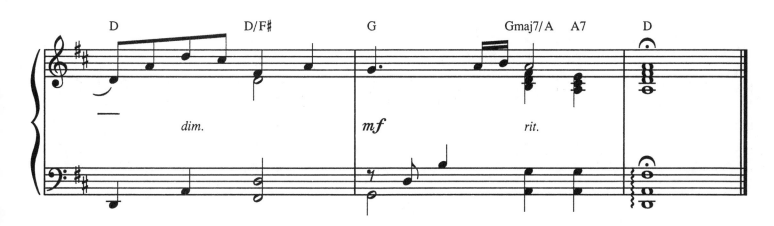

VICTIM OF THE GAME

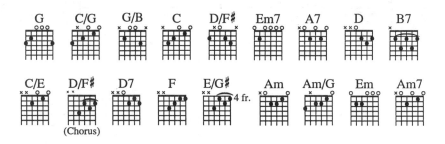

Words and Music by
MARK SANDERS and
GARTH BROOKS

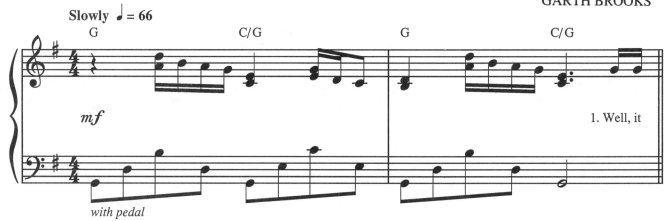

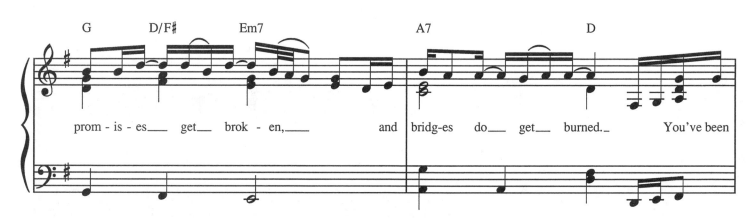

Victim of the Game - 3 - 1

Verse 2:
You were standin' way too close
To see it all fall apart.
And there were things you couldn't hear
'Cause you were listenin' with your heart.
But you can't say I didn't warn you,
Now there's no one else to blame.
There's no one quite as blind
As a victim of the game.
(To Chorus:)

Verse 3:
You know it's really gettin' to you
When you take to tellin' lies.
And you can try to fool your friends
But you can't look 'em in the eye.
There ain't no standin' tall
In the shadow of the shame,
When everybody knows
That you're a victim of the game.
(To Chorus:)

WOLVES

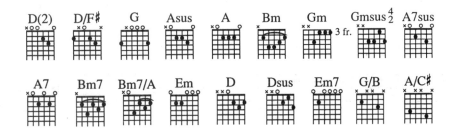

Words and Music by
STEPHANIE DAVIS

D.S. 𝄋 al Coda

Verse 2:
Charlie Barton and his family
Stopped today to say goodbye.
He said the bank was takin' over,
The last few years were just too dry.
And I promised that I'd visit
When they found a place in town.
Then I spent a long time thinkin'
'Bout the ones the wolves pull down.
(To Bridge:)

Verse 3:
Well, I don't mean to be complainin', Lord,
You've always seen me through.
And I know You got your reasons
For each and every thing You do.
But tonight outside my window,
There's a lonesome, mournful sound.
And I just can't keep from thinkin'
'Bout the ones the wolves pull down.

WILD HORSES

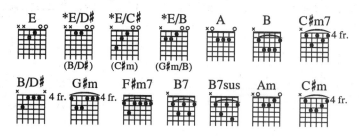

*The guitar should play this chord even though the piano arrangement shows
the chord in parentheses.

Words and Music by
BILL SHORE
and DAVID WILLIS

Wild Horses - 2 - 1

Verse 2:
She'll watch me drive around her block
Gettin' courage up to stop,
To make her one more promise
That I can't keep.
The way I love the rodeo,
I guess I should let her go
Before I hurt her more
Than she loves me.

ROPIN' THE WIND

Against The Grain 146

Burning Bridges 141

Cold Shoulder 162

In Lonesome Dove 166

Papa Loved Mama 152

The River 157

Rodeo 170

Shameless 174

We Bury The Hatchet 180

What She's Doing Now 184

Which One Of Them 188

BURNING BRIDGES

Words and Music by
STEPHANIE C. BROWN
and GARTH BROOKS

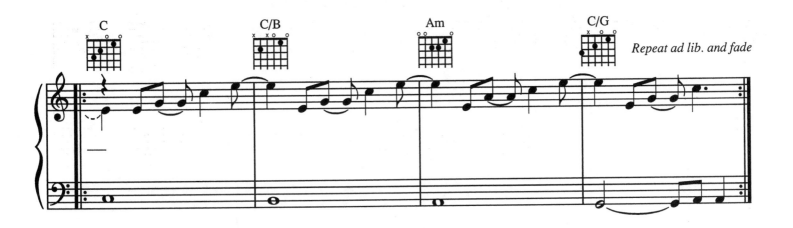

Repeat ad lib. and fade

Verse 2:
Last night we talked of old times,
Families and home towns.
She wondered if we'd both agree
On where we'd settle down.
And I told her that we'd cross that bridge
Whenever it arrived.
Now through the flames I see her,
Standin' on the other side.
(To Chorus:)

AGAINST THE GRAIN

Words and Music by
BRUCE BOUTON, LARRY CORDLE
and CARL JACKSON

Against the Grain - 6 - 1

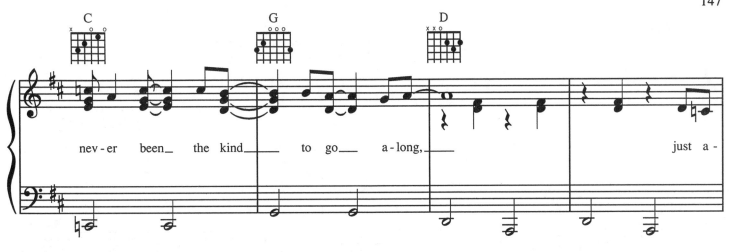

never been_ the kind_ to go_ a - long,_ just a-

-void - in' con - fron - ta - tion for the sake of con - for - ma - tion, and I'll ad -

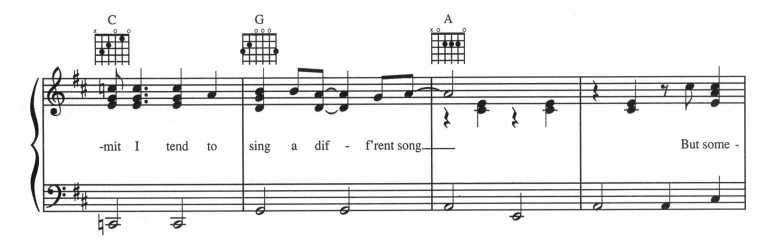

-mit I tend to sing a dif - f'rent song.__ But some -

-times you just_ can't be a - fraid_ to wear a dif - ferent hat.__ If Co -

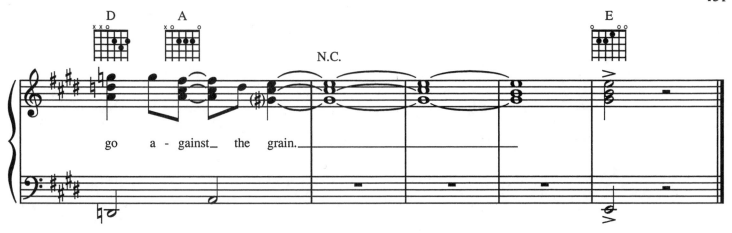

go   a - gainst__   the   grain.__

Verse 2:
Well, I have been accused
Of makin' my own rules;
There must be rebel blood
Just a-runnin' through my veins.
But I ain't no hypocrite,
What you see is what you get,
And that's the only way I know
To play the game.
Old Noah took much ridicule
For building his great ark,
But after forty days and forty nights
He was lookin' pretty smart.
Sometimes it's best to brave the wind and rain,
By havin' strength to go against the grain.

PAPA LOVED MAMA

Fast blues feel ♩ = 160

Words and Music by
KIM WILLIAMS and GARTH BROOKS

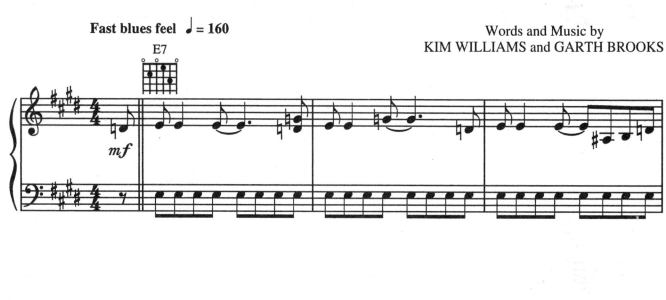

D.S. 𝄋 al Coda

2. Well, it was_ hit the brakes_ and he was shift-ing gears._ Ma-

⊕ *Coda*

Ma-ma's in the grave-yard, Pa - pa's in the pen.

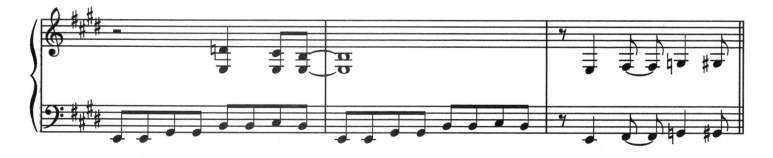

Verse 2:

Well, it was bound to happen and one night it did,
Papa came home and it was just us kids.
He had a dozen roses and a bottle of wine,
If he was lookin' to surprise us, he was doin' fine.
I heard him cry for Mama up and down the hall,
Then I heard a bottle break against the bedroom wall.
That old diesel engine made an eerie sound,
When papa fired it up and headed into town.

Chorus 2:

Well, the picture in the paper showed the scene real well,
Papa's rig was buried in the local motel.
The desk clerk said he saw it all real clear.
He never hit the brakes and he was shifting gears.
(To Chorus 1:)

THE RIVER

Words and Music by
VICTORIA SHAW and GARTH BROOKS

The River - 5 - 1

The River - 5 - 3

(1st time only)

Verse 2:
Too many times we stand aside
And let the waters slip away
'Til what we put off 'til tomorrow
Has now become today.
So, don't you sit upon the shoreline
And say you're satisfied.
Choose to chance the rapids
And dare to dance the tide. Yes, I will . . .
(To Chorus:)

COLD SHOULDER

Words and Music by
KENT BLAZY, KIM WILLIAMS
and GARTH BROOKS

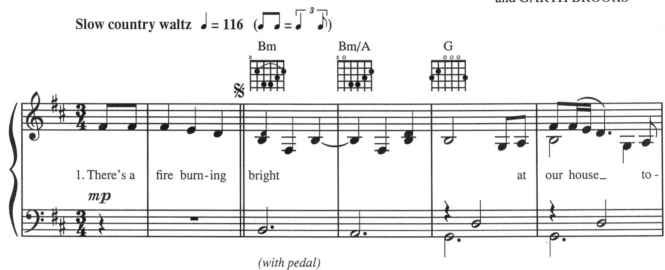

1. There's a fire burn-ing bright at our house to-

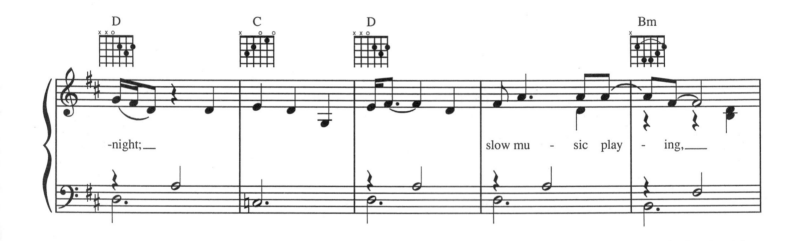

-night;___ slow mu - sic play - ing,___

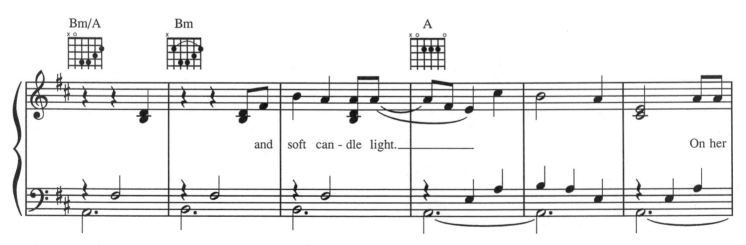

and soft can - dle light.___ On her

Cold Shoulder - 4 - 1

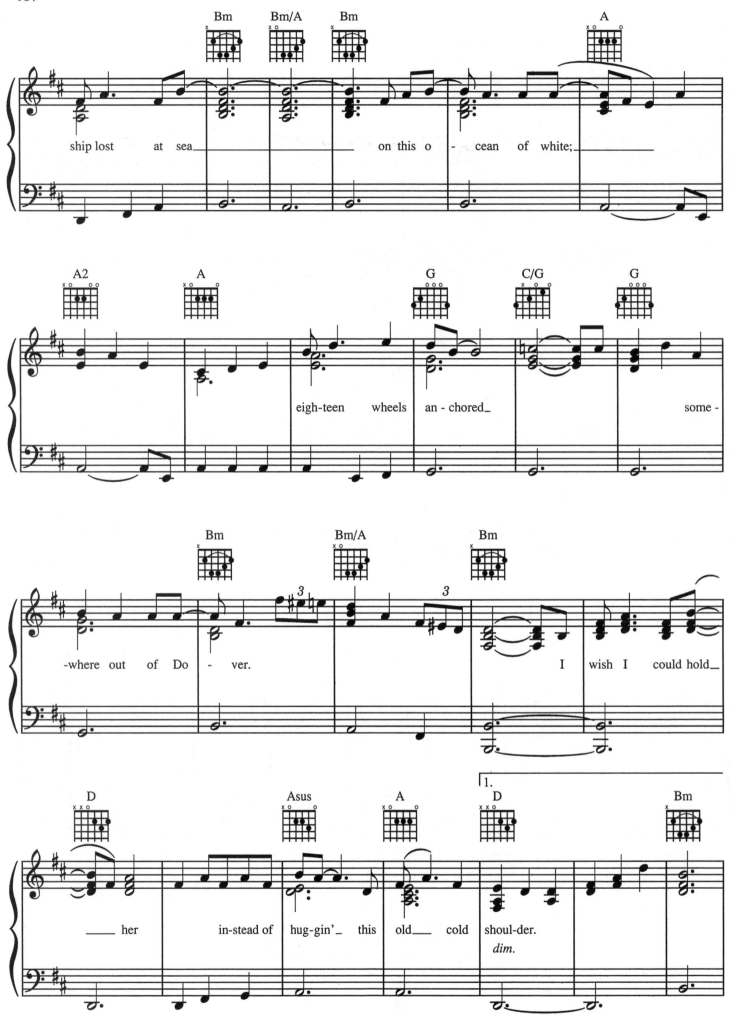

Verse 2:
This old highway is like a woman sometimes;
She can be your best friend, but she's the real jealous kind.
She's the lady that leads me to the life I dream of.
She's the mistress that keeps me from the ones that I love.
(To Chorus:)

IN LONESOME DOVE

Moderately ♩ = 82

Words and Music by
CYNTHIA LIMBAUGH
and GARTH BROOKS

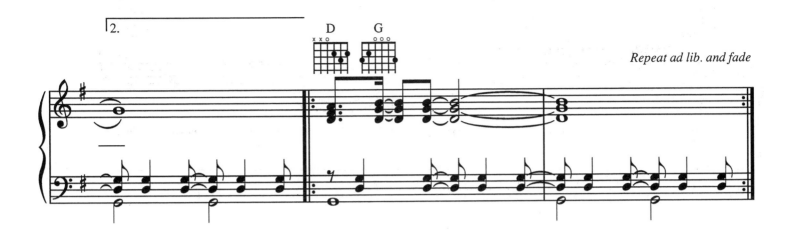

Repeat ad lib. and fade

Verse 2:

A farmer's daughter with a gentle hand,
A blooming rose in a bed of sand;
She loved the man who wore a star,
A Texas Ranger known near and far.
So they got married and they had a child.
But times were tough and the West was wild.
So it was no surprise the day she learned
That her Texas man would not return
To Lonesome Dove. *(To Chorus:)*

Verse 3:

She watched her boy grow to a man.
He had an angel's heart and the devil's hand.
He wore his star for all to see.
He was a Texas lawman legacy.
Then one day word blew into town.
It seemed the men that shot his father down
Had robbed a bank in Cherico.
The only thing 'tween them and Mexico
Was Lonesome Dove. *(To Verse 4:)*

Verse 4:

The shadows stretched across the land
As the shots rang out down the Rio Grande.
And when the smoke had finally cleared the street,
The men lay at the ranger's feet.
But legend tells to this very day
That shots were comin' from an alleyway.
'Though no one knows who held the gun,
There ain't no doubt if you ask someone
In Lonesome Dove. *(To Chorus:)*

RODEO

Words and Music by
LARRY BASTIAN

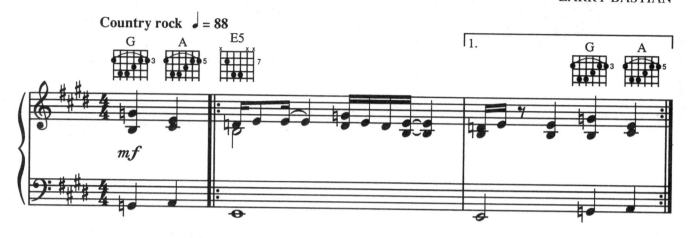

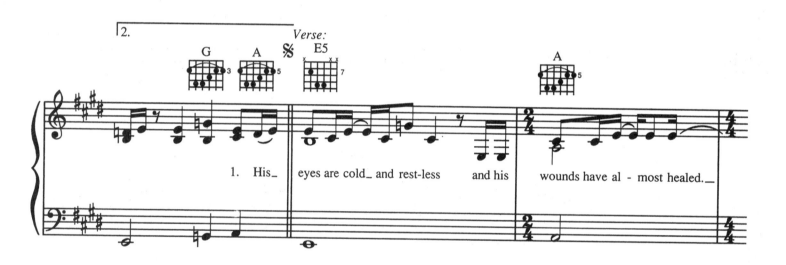

Rodeo - 4 - 1

172

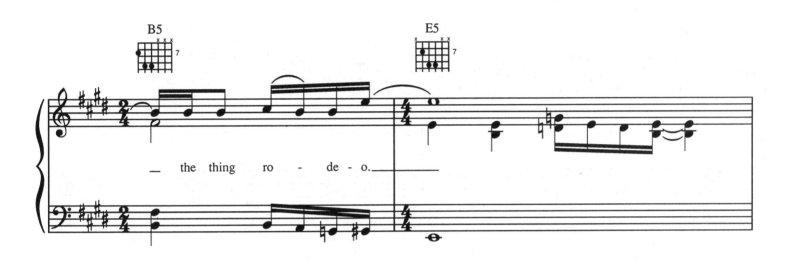

Verse 2:
She does her best to hold him
When his love comes to call.
But his need for it controls him
And her back's against the wall.
And it's "So long, girl, I'll see you.",
When it's time for him to go.
You know the woman wants her cowboy
Like he wants his rodeo.
(To Chorus:)

Verse 3:
It'll drive a cowboy crazy,
It'll drive the man insane.
And he'll sell off everything he owns
Just to pay to play her game.
And a broken home and some broken bones
Is all he'll have to show
For all the years that he spent chasin'
This dream they call rodeo.
(To Chorus:)

SHAMELESS

Words and Music by
BILLY JOEL

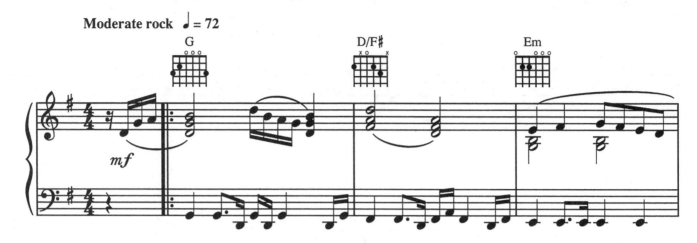

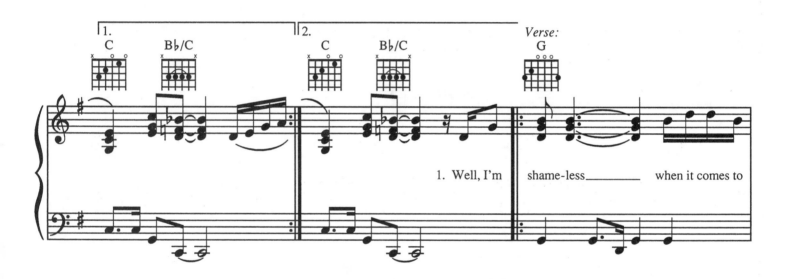

1. Well, I'm shame-less_____ when it comes to

lov - ing you._ I'll do an - y-thing you want_ me to,_____ I'll do an - y-thing at

Shameless - 6 - 1

fool.   I just want-ed you to   know._____   I'm

Verse 2:
I'm shameless, oh honey, I don't have a prayer.
Every time I see you standing there,
I go down upon my knees.
And I'm changing, swore I'd never compromise.
Oh, but you convinced me otherwise.
I'll do anything you please.
You see, in all my life I've never found
What I couldn't resist, what I couldn't turn down.
I could walk away from anyone I ever knew,
But I can't walk away from you.
(To Bridge:)

WE BURY THE HATCHET

Words and Music by
WADE KIMES
and **GARTH BROOKS**

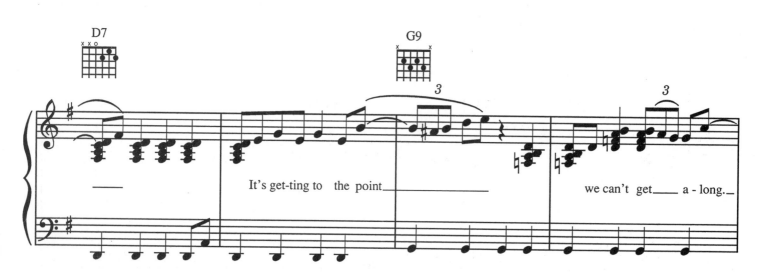

We Bury the Hatchet - 4 - 1

Verse 2:
Well, I was kissing on Cindy.
Hey, that I won't deny.
But that's a long time ago;
I let a dead dog lie.

But if you want to cut deep,
How 'bout you and ol' Joe?
I caught you down at the creek
Just ten years ago.
(To Chorus:)

We Bury the Hatchet - 4 - 4

WHAT SHE'S DOING NOW

Words and Music by
PAT ALGER and GARTH BROOKS

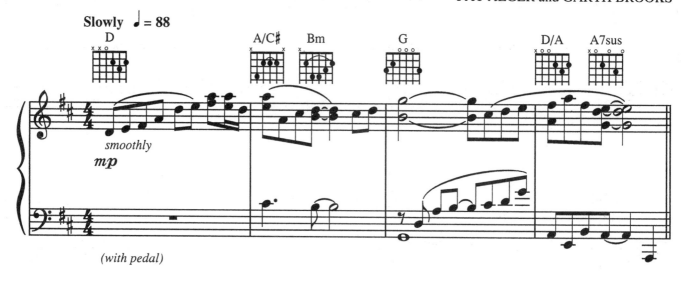

Slowly ♩ = 88

smoothly

mp

(with pedal)

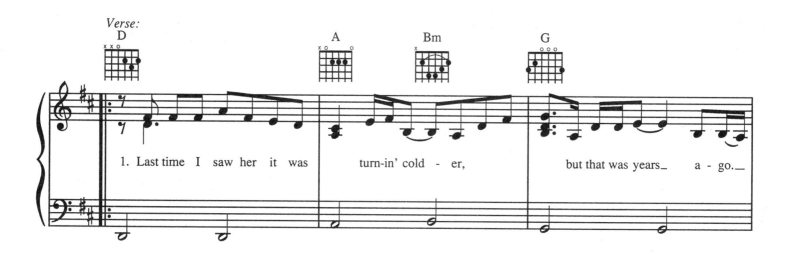

Verse:

1. Last time I saw her it was   turn-in' cold - er,   but that was years_ a - go._

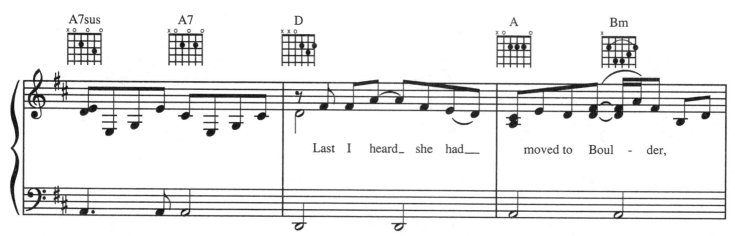

Last I heard_ she had__ moved to Boul - der,

What She's Doing Now - 4 - 1

186

mind_____ and emp-ty-ing__ my heart. I can hear_ her call_____ each time the cold_ wind

blows. And I won-der if___ she knows_____ what she's do-in' now.

mp

that what she's do - in' now___

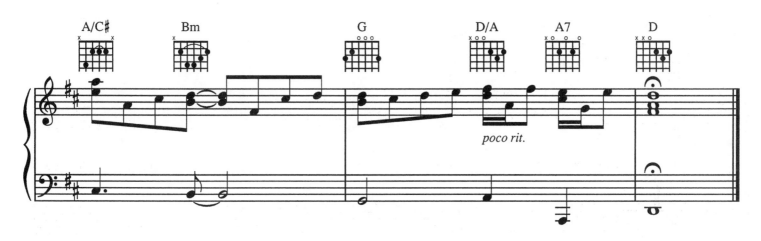

Verse 2:
Just for laughs, I dialed her old number,
But no one knew her name.
Hung up the phone, sat there and wondered
If she'd ever done the same.
I took a walk in the evenin' wind
To clear my head somehow.
But tonight I lie here thinkin'
What's she doin' now.
(To Chorus:)

WHICH ONE OF THEM

Words and Music by
GARTH BROOKS

Which One of Them - 3 - 1

Which One of Them - 3 - 2

190

GARTH BROOKS

The Chase

Dixie Chicken...192

Every Now And Then 196

Face To Face..210

Learning To Live Again 199

Mr. Right..202

Night Rider's Lament...214

Something With A Ring To It...............................205

Somewhere Other Than The Night....................220

That Summer..226

Walking After Midnight 236

We Shall Be Free 231

DIXIE CHICKEN

Words and Music by
LOWELL GEORGE and
MARTIN KIBBEE

Dixie Chicken - 4 - 1

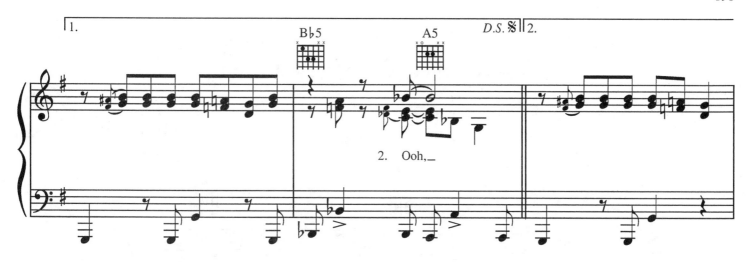

Verse 2:
Ooh, we hit all the hotspots,
And my money flowed like wine,
Till the lowdown southern whiskey
Began to fog my mind.
Well, I don't remember church bells,
Or the money I put down
On the white picket fence and boardwalk
At the house on the edge of town.
Now, but boy do I remember
The strain of her refrain,
And the nights we spent together
And the way she called my name.
(To Chorus:)

Verse 3:
It's been a year since she ran away.
Guess that guitar player sure could play.
She always like to sing along;
He was always handy with a song.
Then one night in the lobby
Of the Commodore Hotel,
I by chance met a bartender
Who said he knew her well.
And as he handed me a drink,
He began to hum a song,
And all the boys there at the bar
Began to sing along:
(To Chorus:)

EVERY NOW AND THEN

Words and Music by
BUDDY MONDLOCK and
GARTH BROOKS

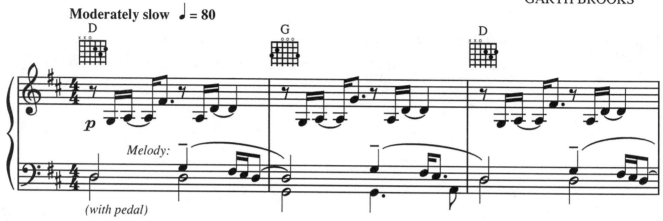

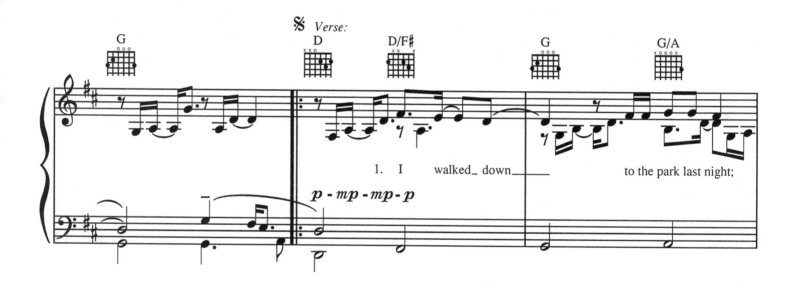

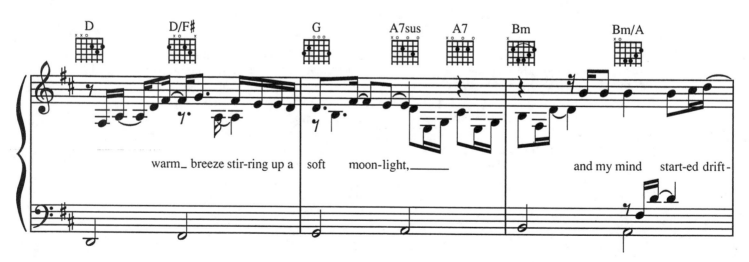

Every Now and Then - 3 - 1

Verse 2:
The other day, I saw a car like you used to drive;
I got a funny feeling down deep inside,
And for the briefest moment, I felt a smile begin.
Yes I do think about you every now and then.
(To Chorus:)

Verse 3:
I heard a song on the radio just yesterday,
The same one you always asked me to play.
And when the song was over, I wished they'd played it again.
Yes I do think about you every now and then.
(To Chorus:)

Verse 4:
I've been layin' here all night, listening to the rain,
Talkin' to my heart and trying to explain
Why sometimes I catch myself wondering what might have been.
Yes I do think about you every now and then.
(To Coda:)

LEARNING TO LIVE AGAIN

Words and Music by
DON SCHLITZ and
STEPHANIE DAVIS

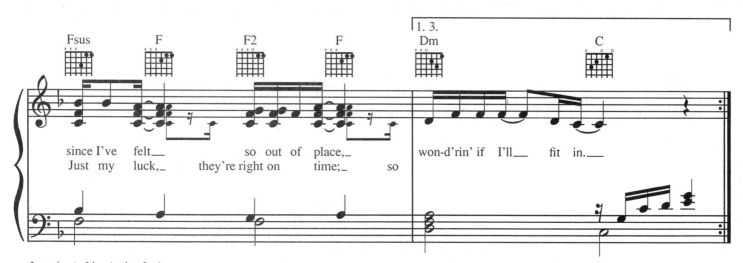

Learning to Live Again - 3 - 1

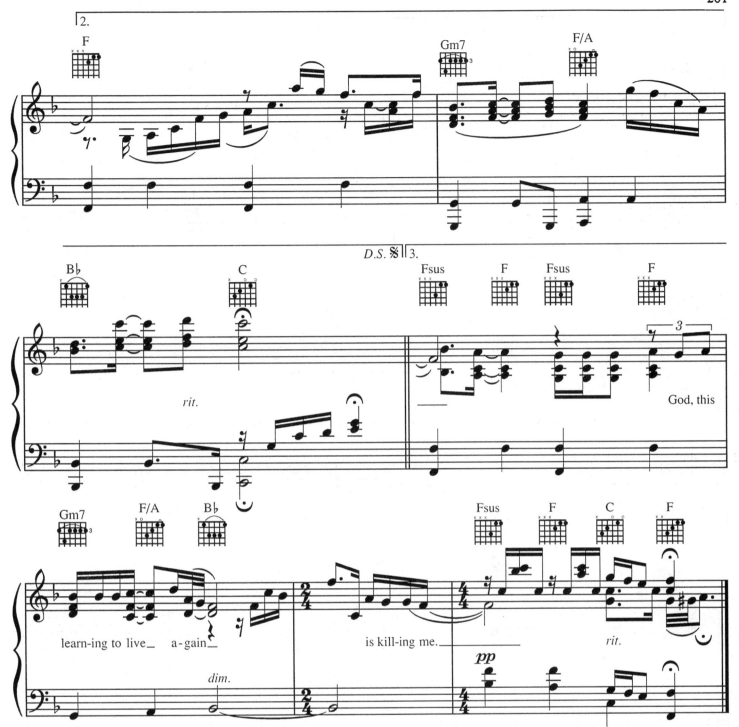

Verse 3:
Little cafe, table for four,
But there's just conversation for three.
I like the way she let me get the door;
I wonder what she thinks of me.

Verse 4:
Debbie just whispered, "You're doing fine."
And I wish that I felt the same.
She's asked me to dance; now her hand's in mine;
Oh my God, I've forgotten her name. *(To Chorus:)*

Chorus 2:
But I'm gonna smile my best smile,
And I'm gonna laugh like it's going out of style,
Look into her eyes, and pray that she don't see
This learning to live again is killing me.

Verse 5:
Now here we are beneath her porch light,
And I say what a great time it's been;
A kiss on the cheek, a whisper goodnight,
And I say, "Can I see you again?"

Chorus 3:
And she just smiles her best smile,
And she laughs like it's goin' out of style,
Looks into my eyes, and says, "We'll see."
Oh, this learning to live again is killing me.
God, this learning to live again is killing me.

Learning to Live Again - 3 - 3

MR. RIGHT

Words and Music by
GARTH BROOKS

Verse 2:
And if you'd choose to be my wife,
I would love you all my life.
I'd do everything your precious heart allowed.
Or we could make love all night long,
And in the morning, I'd be gone.
I'm Mr. Right, or Mr. Right Now.
(To Chorus:)

SOMETHING WITH A RING TO IT

Words and Music by
AARON TIPPIN and MARK COLLIE

206

Something With a Ring to It - 5 - 3

Something With a Ring to It - 5 - 5

FACE TO FACE

Words and Music by
TONY ARATA

your glass-es, the girls all laughed_ as he pushed_ you to_ the floor,_ un-til you

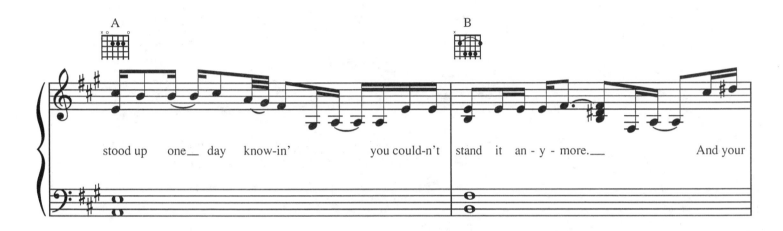

stood up one_ day know-in' you could-n't stand it an-y-more._ And your

gen-tle hand_ was fi-n'lly clenched_ in_ rage,_ and you were face to_ face._

Chorus 1 & 3:

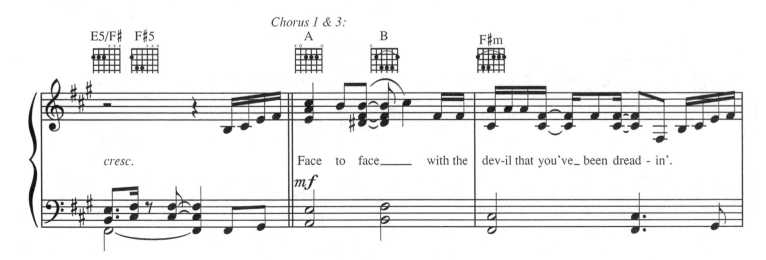

cresc. Face to face_ with the dev-il that you've_ been dread-in'.

Face to Face - 4 - 2

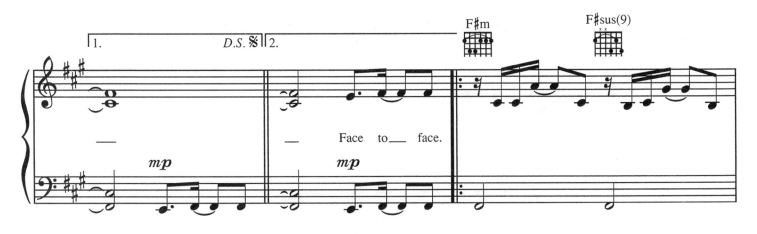

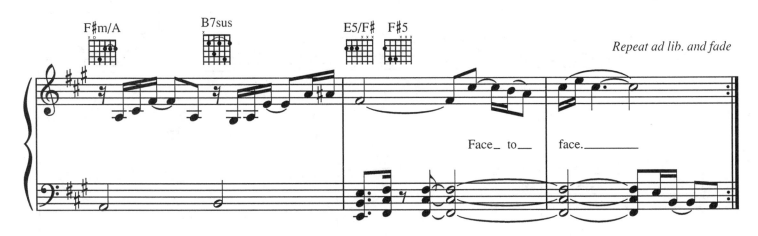

Verse 2:
Your date showed up with flowers,
And you thought your prayers had come.
But with every passing hour,
You watched it come undone.
Then the night exploded and you begged him no,
But he forever changed your life.
And now, he waits a judge and jury,
Thinkin' you'll break down inside.
And with a finger you can put his fists away,
And you're face to face.

Chorus 2:
Face to face with the devil that you've been dreadin'.
Eye to eye finally has arrived.
But bad as it was, well, now sister, wasn't it better
Dealin' with him face to face?

Verse 3:
Drivin' by the grave yard
On a wicked winter's eve,
And you're wonderin' why a man of faith
Is whistlin' nervously.
Then you stop the car
And you hold your heart,
'Cause you finally realize—
Hell, the devil ain't in the darkness,
He's a-rattlin' 'round inside.
And with folded hands you truly start to pray,
'Cause you're face to face.
(To Chorus:)

NIGHT RIDER'S LAMENT

Words and Music by
MICHAEL BURTON

Chorus:

"Why___ do you ride_____ for your mon-ey?___ Tell me, why___ do you rope_ for short pay?_____ You ain't a - get-tin'___ no - where___ and you're los - in' your___ share._____ Boy, you must have gone cra - zy out___ there.

1. 2. He said,___ Ah, but they've_

cresc.

Verse 2:
He said, "Last night, I ran on to Jenny,
And she's married and she has a good life.
Boy, you sure missed the track when you never came back.
She's the perfect professional's wife."

Chorus 2:
And she asked me, "Why does he ride for his money?
Tell me, why does he rope for short pay?
He ain't a-gettin' nowhere and he's losin' his share.
Boy, he must have gone crazy out there."

SOMEWHERE OTHER THAN THE NIGHT

Words and Music by
KENT BLAZY and
GARTH BROOKS

Somewhere Other Than the Night - 6 - 1

THAT SUMMER

Words and Music by
PAT ALGER, SANDY MAHL
and GARTH BROOKS

own.__
while.__

We were a thou-sand miles from no-where,
There was a dif-f'rence in her laugh-ter;

wheat fields as far as I could see,_____
there was a soft-ness in her eyes;_____

both need-in' some-thin' from each
and on the air, there was a

oth - er,
hung-er

not know-in' yet what that might be.
e - ven a boy could rec - og - nize.

1.

2. 3. 4.

Chorus:

2. Till she came_ to me one

1. 3. She had a need to feel the thun-der,_____

cresc.

f

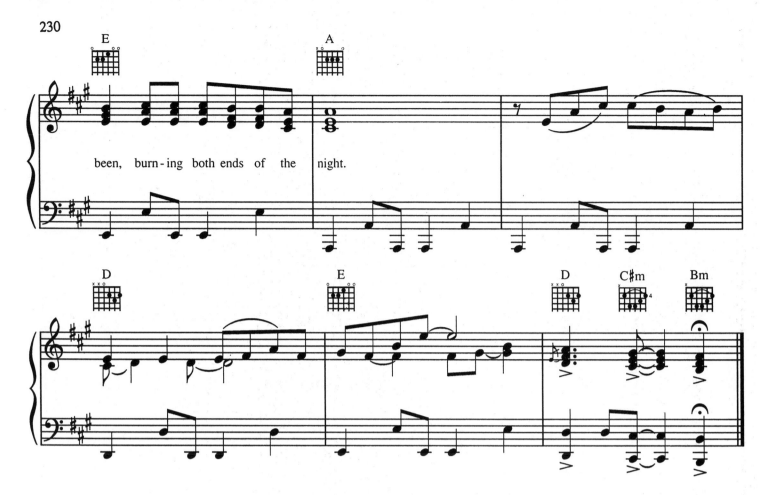

been, burn-ing both ends of the night.

Verse 3:

That summer wind was all around me;
Nothin' between us but the night.
And when I told her that I'd never,
She softly whispered, "That's alright."
And then I watched her hands of leather
Turn to velvet in a touch.
There's never been another summer
When I have ever learned so much.

Chorus 2:

We had a need to feel the thunder,
To chase the lightning from the skies,
To watch the storm, with all its wonder
Raging in each other's eyes.
We had to ride the heat of passion,
Like a comet burnin' bright,
Rushing headlong in the wind,
Out where only dreams had been,
Burnin' both ends of the night.

Verse 4:

I often think about that summer:
The sweat, the moonlight, and the lace.
And I have rarely held another
When I haven't seen her face.
And every time I pass a wheat field,
And watch it dancin' with the wind,
Although I know it isn't real,
I just can't help but feel
Her hungry arms again.

Chorus 3: Repeat Chorus 1, then to Coda.

WE SHALL BE FREE

Words and Music by
STEPHANIE DAVIS and GARTH BROOKS

We Shall Be Free - 5 - 1

234

We Shall Be Free - 5 - 4

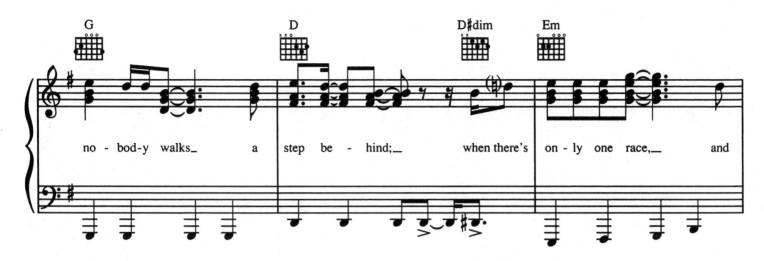

no - bod-y walks_ a step be - hind;_ when there's on - ly one race,_ and

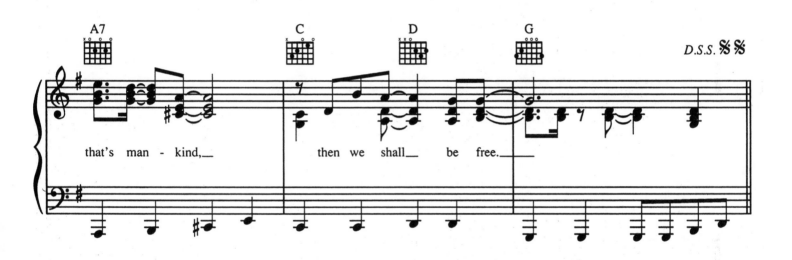

that's man - kind,_ then we shall_ be free._

D.S.S. 𝄋 𝄋

Verse 3:
When we're free to love anyone we choose,
When this world's big enough for all different views,
When we all can worship from our own kind of pew,
Then we shall be free.
(To Chorus:)

Chorus 2:
We shall be free,
We shall be free.
Have a little faith, hold out,
'Cause we shall be free.
(To Bridge:)

Chorus 3:
We shall be free,
We shall be free.
Stand straight, (walk proud,)
Have a little faith, (hold out;)
We shall be free.

Chorus 4:
We shall be free,
We shall be free.
(Stand straight,) stand straight,
(Have a little faith,) walk proud,
'Cause we shall be free.

Chorus 5:
Repeat Chorus 1 and fade

WALKING AFTER MIDNIGHT

Lyrics by
DON HECHT

Music by
ALAN BLOCK

Walking after Midnight - 4 - 1

238

239

Walking after Midnight - 4 - 4

IN PIECES

Ain't Going Down ('Til The Sun Comes Up)...241

American Honky-Tonk Bar Association 280

Anonymous...286

Callin' Baton Rouge 256

The Cowboy Song 246

Kickin' And Screamin'..................................251

The Night I Called The Old Man Out 262

The Night Will Only Know............................268

One Night A Day...272

The Red Strokes...276

Standing Outside The Fire.............................290

AIN'T GOING DOWN
('Til the Sun Comes Up)

Words and Music by
KENT BLAZY, KIM WILLIAMS and
GARTH BROOKS

Rock ♩ = 168

Verse 1 & 2:

1. Six o'-clock on Fri-day eve-ning, Ma-ma does-n't know she's leav-ing

'til she hears the screen door slam-ming, rub-ber squeal-in', gears a-jam-ming.

Ain't Going Down ('Til the Sun Comes Up) - 5 - 1

242

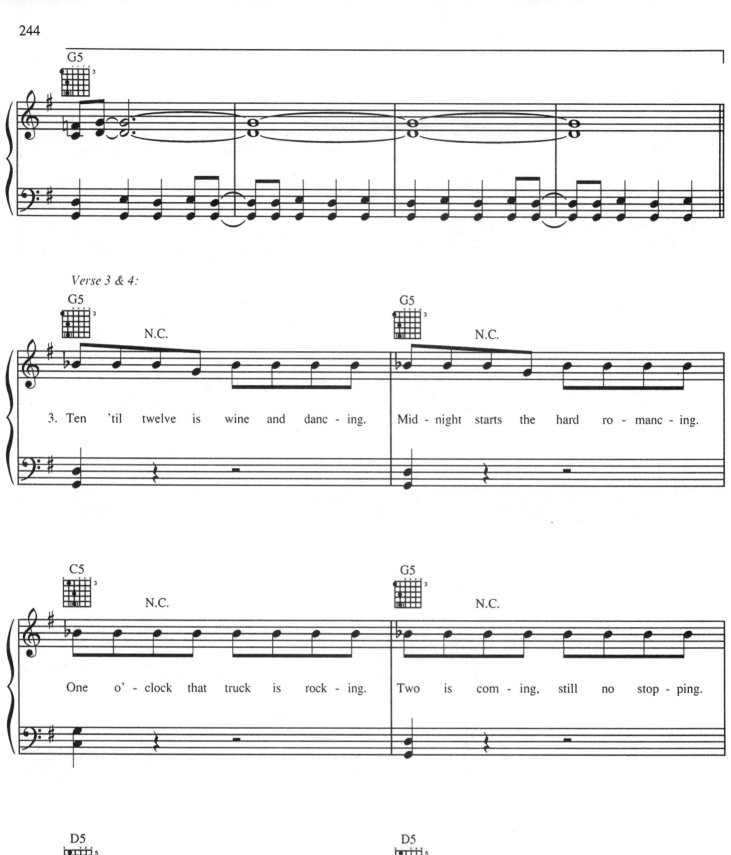

Verse 3 & 4:

G5   N.C.   G5   N.C.

3. Ten 'til twelve is wine and danc - ing. Mid - night starts the hard ro - manc - ing.

C5   N.C.   G5   N.C.

One o' - clock that truck is rock - ing. Two is com - ing, still no stop - ping.

D5   N.C.   D5   N.C.

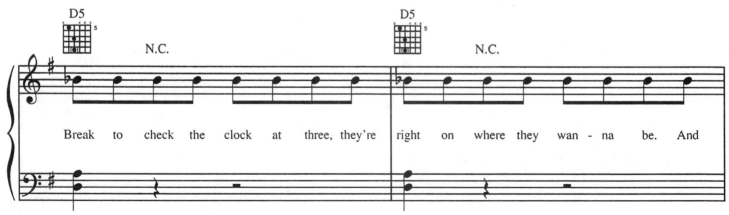

Break to check the clock at three, they're right on where they wan - na be. And

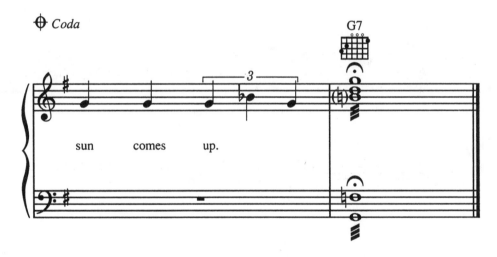

Verse 2:
Nine o'clock the show is ending,
But the fun is just beginning.
She knows he's anticipating
But she's gonna keep him waiting.
Grab a bite to eat
And then they're headin' to the honky tonk,
But loud crowds and line dancing
Just ain't what they really want.
Drive out to the boondocks and park down by the creek,
And where it's George Strait 'til real late
And dancing cheek to cheek.
(To Chorus:)

Verse 4:
Six o'clock on Saturday
Her folks don't know he's on his way.
The stalls are clean, the horses fed,
They say she's grounded 'til she's dead.
And here he comes around the bend,
Slowing down, she's jumping in.
Hey, Mom! Your daughter's gone
And there they go again.
(To Chorus:)

THE COWBOY SONG

Moderately slow two-beat ♩ = 72

Words and Music by
ROY ROBINSON

(with pedal)

Verses 1 & 2:

1. Push-in' horns__ weren't eas - y like__ the mov - ie said it was, and I don't re-call__ no dance__ hall girls or ho- -tel rooms__ with rugs._____ You worked hot and tired__ and nas-

*L.H. tacet 1st Verse on recording.

The Cowboy Song - 5 - 1

Verses 3, 4, etc.:

3. (Instrumental solo . . .
(4.) when you see___ the cow - boy, he's not rag - ged by___ his choice.___ He
5.6.etc. *(Instrumental solo ad lib.)*

nev - er meant___ to bow___ them legs___ or put that___ grav - el in his voice.___

___ He's just chas - in' what___ he real - ly loves___ and what's

burn - in' in___ his soul, wish-in' to God that he'd___ been born a hun-

1.

. . . end solo) 4. So

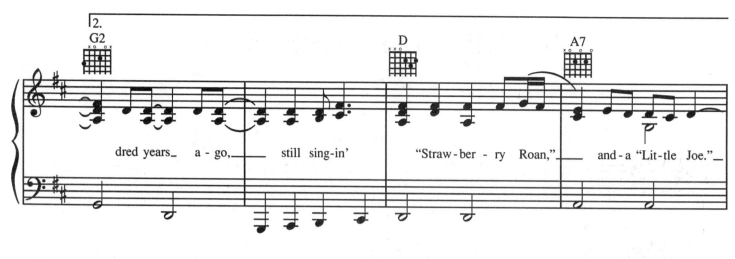

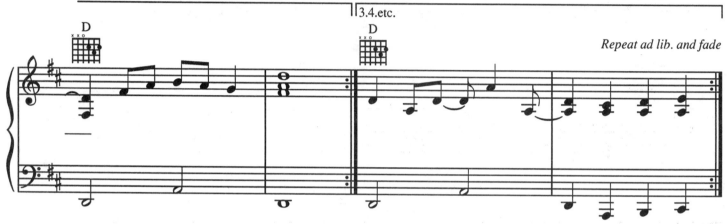

Repeat ad lib. and fade

Verse 2:
Like the time we hit the river,
And the rains began to fall,
And the water was risin' so damn fast,
We thought it'd drown us all.
We lost a lot of steers that day,
And four or five good mounts.
But when all the boys rode into camp,
We knew that's what counts,
And we sang, "Yippee Ti Yi Yay" and "Amazing Grace."
(To Bridge:)

KICKIN' AND SCREAMIN'

Moderate blues swing ♩ = 92

Words and Music by
TONY ARATA

1. Well,__ I don't know__ what my un-cle did,__ but he must have__ done it right.__ They__ sure strung him up__ one__ Sat-ur-day night. He__ had spent his whole_ life fuss-in',_____ would have

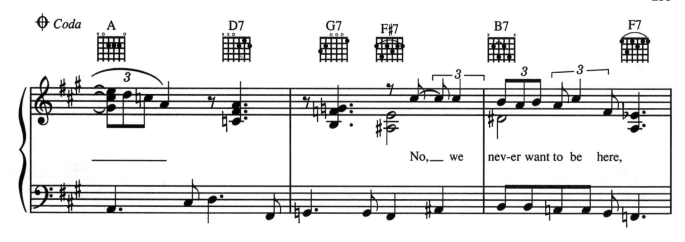

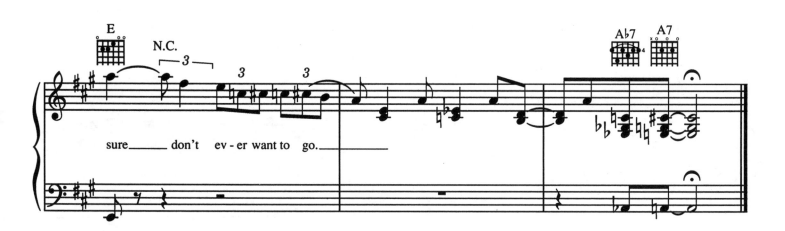

Verse 2:
Well, I could hear those church bells ringin'.
To my best friend I was clingin',
Screamin', "If you love me brother don't let me go."
Well, then the whole scene was repeated
Two years later, I begged and pleaded
Screamin; "If you love me, honey,
Now you know you wouldn't want to let me go."
No, I didn't want to do it,
But I sure don't want to see it come undone.
(To Chorus:)

CALLIN' BATON ROUGE

Moderately fast ♩ = 112

Words and Music by
DENNIS LINDE

Verse:

1. I spent last night in the arms of a girl in Lou - i - si - an - a,

and though I'm out on the high - way,__ my thoughts__ are still with her.__

Callin' Baton Rouge - 6 - 1

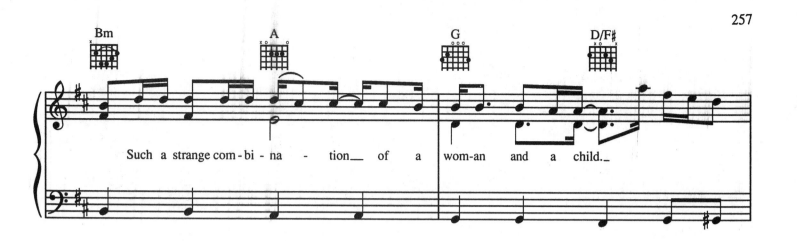

Such a strange com-bi-na - tion__ of a wom-an and a child.__

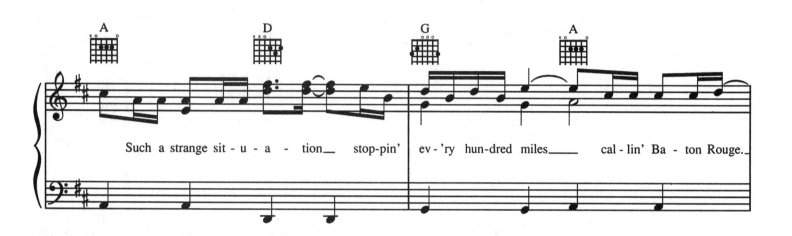

Such a strange sit - u - a - tion__ stop-pin' ev - 'ry hun-dred miles_____ cal - lin' Ba - ton Rouge.__

1.

Chorus:

Op - er - a - tor, won't you put me on through? I got - ta send my love down to Ba - ton Rouge._

Hur - ry up; won't you put her on the line? I got - ta talk to the girl just - a one more time.__

(Instrumental solo . . .

Chorus:

er - a - tor, won't you put me on through? I got - ta send my love down to Ba - ton Rouge._ Hur -

- ry up; won't you put her on the line? I got - ta talk to the girl just - a one more time._

Call - in' Ba - ton Rouge._

Op -

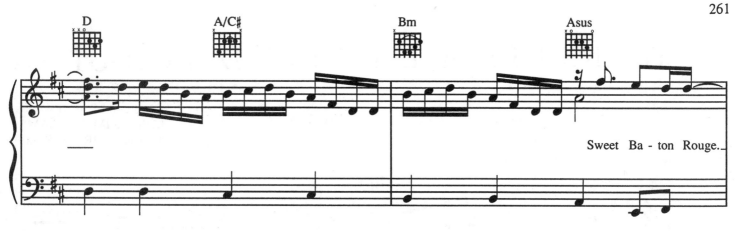

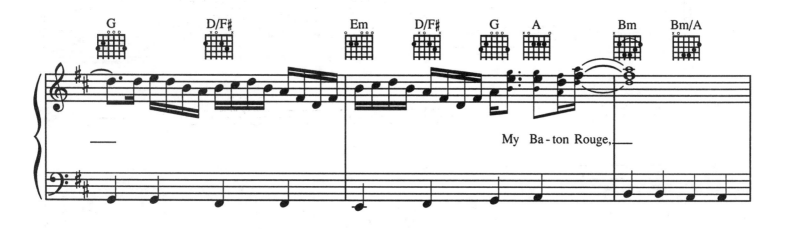

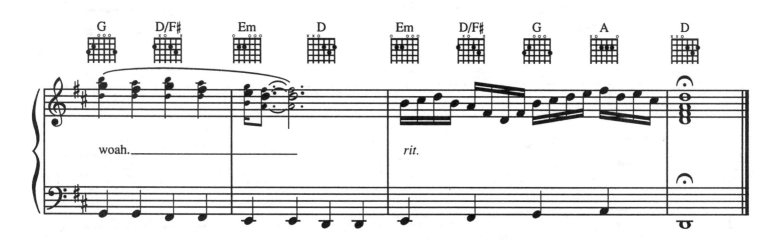

Verse 2:
A replay of last night's events
Roll through my mind,
Except a scene or two
Erased by sweet red wine.
And I see a truck stop sign ahead,
So I change lanes.
I need a cup of coffee,
And a couple dollars change,
Callin' Baton Rouge.
(To Chorus:)

Callin' Baton Rouge - 6 - 6

THE NIGHT I CALLED THE OLD MAN OUT

Words and Music by
PAT ALGER, KIM WILLIAMS
and GARTH BROOKS

Fast driving beat ♩ = 168

%% *Verse:*

1. The din-ing room fell si-lent; I can't be-lieve what I just said.

The Night I Called the Old Man Out - 6 - 1

I just told___ my dad he's full of it, and I watched his face___ turn red.___ Well, then I should-'ve said___ "I'm sor-ry,"___ but I matched him shout___ to shout.___ I can still

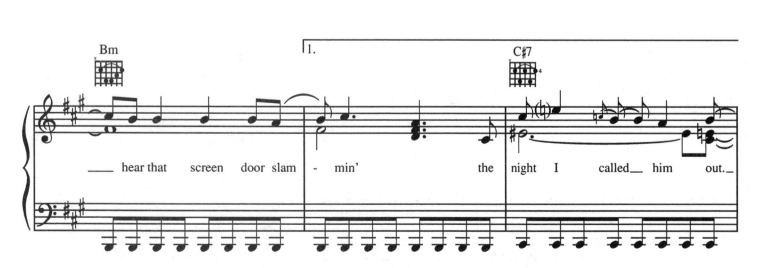

___ hear that screen door slam-min' the night I called___ him out.___

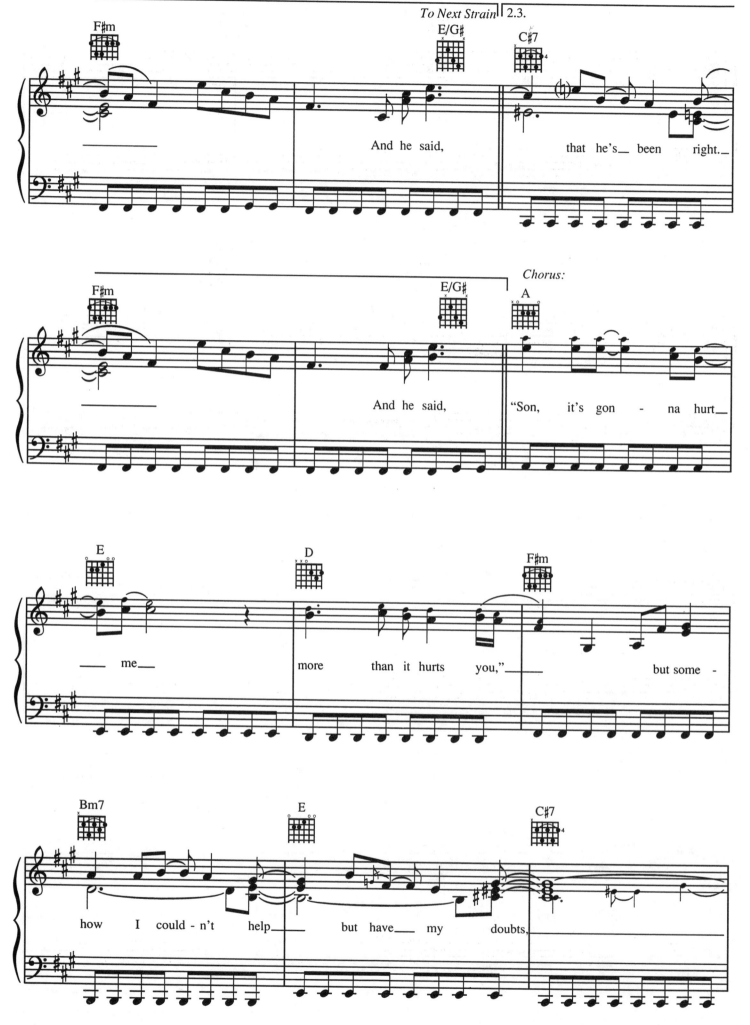

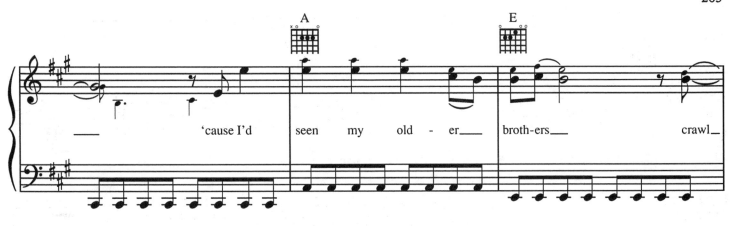

'cause I'd seen my old - er___ broth-ers___ crawl___

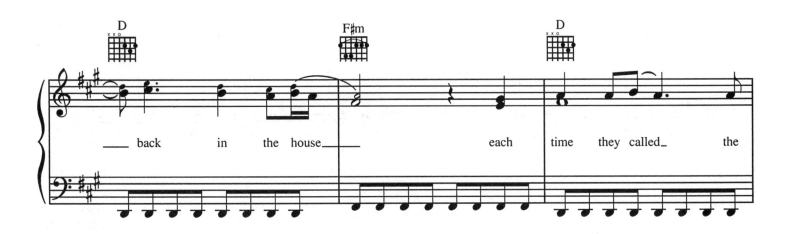

___ back in the house___ each time they called___ the

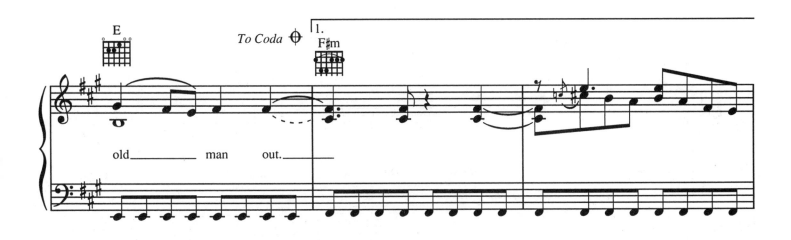

To Coda ⊕ |1.

old___ man out.___

D.S. 𝄋 ||2.

The Night I Called the Old Man out - 6 - 4

D.S. 𝄋 *al Coda*

3. It was

⊕ *Coda*

Just   like   my   old - er____

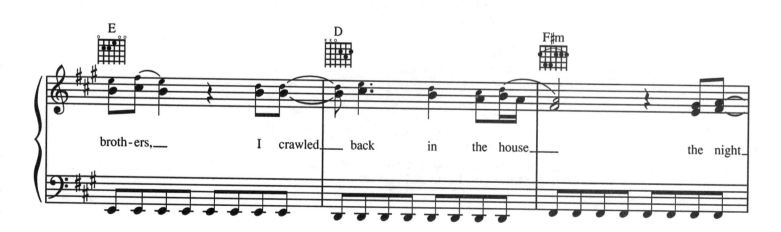

broth-ers,____   I crawled____ back   in   the house____   the night____

The Night I Called the Old Man out - 6 - 5

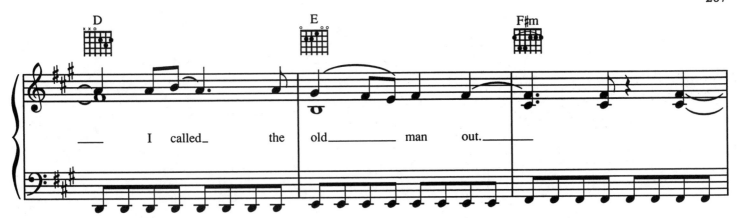

I called the old man out.

Verse 2:
Fist to fist and eye to eye,
Standin' toe to toe;
He would've let me walk away,
But I just would not let it go.
Years of my frustration
Had lead me to this night.
Now, he'll pay for all the
Times that he's been right.
(To Chorus:)

Verse 3:
It was over in a minute.
That's when I realized
The blood came from my mouth and nose,
But the tears came from his eyes.
And in memory of that fateful night,
I know the greatest pain was his,
And I just pray some day
I'm half the man he is.
(To Chorus:)

THE NIGHT WILL ONLY KNOW

Words and Music by
STEPHANIE DAVIS, JENNY YATES
and GARTH BROOKS

The Night Will Only Know - 4 - 1

grip of fate__ had tight-ened____ and with trem-bling hands_ they wiped_ a-way_____ the steam.
man-y pills__ were tak-en_____ and they ruled the wom-an's death_ a su - i-cide.__

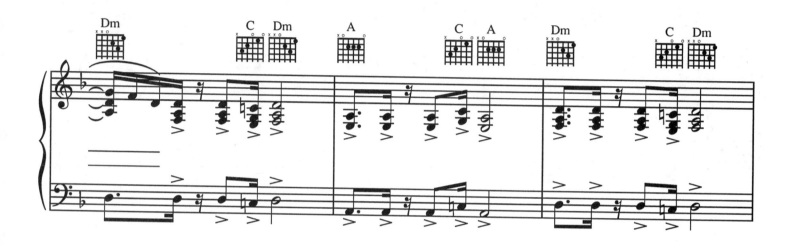

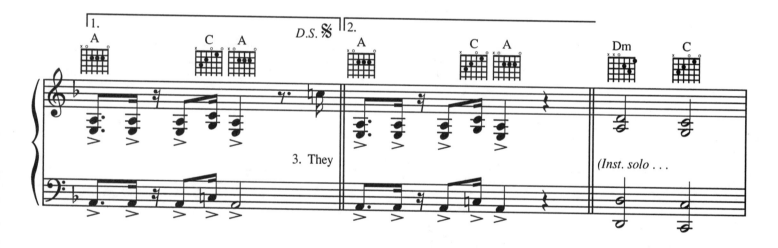

3. They

(Inst. solo . . .

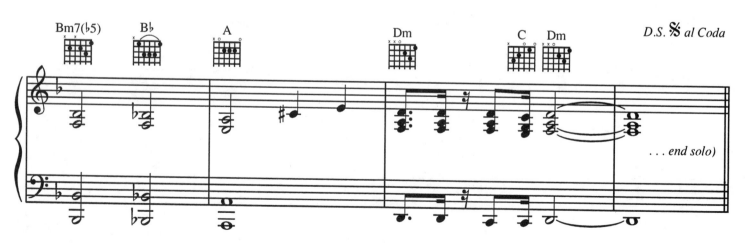

. . . end solo)

The Night Will Only Know - 4 - 3

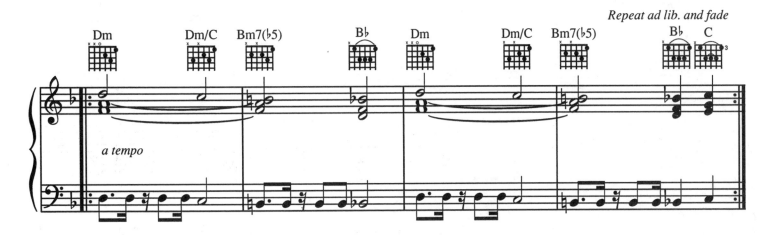

Verse 2:
Parked on some old backstreet,
They laid down in the backseat
And fell into the fire down below.
But they would pay for their deceiving
For a deadly web was weaving.
Why they picked that spot that evening
Lord, the night will only know.
(To Chorus:)

Verse 3:
They saw a woman pleading,
Stumbling, begging and retreating,
'Til she became the victim of her foe.
And they watched her fall in silence
To save their own alliance.
But the reason for the violence
Just the night will only know.
(To Chorus:)

Verse 4:
Bound by their behavior,
They could have been her savior.
Now guilt becomes the endless debt they owe.
But another crime was committed
And it's never been admitted.
Have the guilty been acquitted?
Lord, the night will only know.
(To Coda)

ONE NIGHT A DAY

Words and Music by
GARY BURR and PETE WASNER

One Night a Day - 4 - 1

275

Verse 2:
I'm callin' every friend I've had,
I wake 'em up, and make 'em mad,
To let 'em know that I'm ok.
I used to sit and talk to you.
They're all just a substitute
To get through one night a day.
(To Chorus:)

Chorus 2:
One night a day, one step away
From leavin' you behind.
I stay up with the late, late show,
Just another way I know
To get through one night a day,
To get through one night a day.

THE RED STROKES

Words and Music by
JAMES GARVER, LISA SANDERSON,
JENNY YATES and GARTH BROOKS

*L.H. tacet 1st Verse on recording.

The Red Strokes - 4 - 1

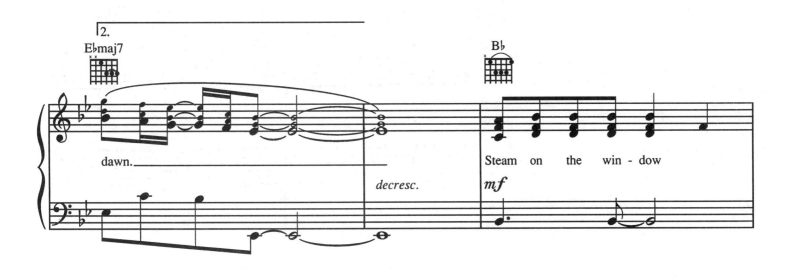

Verse 2:
Steam on the window, Salt in a kiss:
Two hearts have never pounded like this.
Inspired by a vision
That they can't command,
Erasing the borders
With each brush of a hand.
(To Chorus:)

AMERICAN HONKY-TONK BAR ASSOCIATION

Words and Music by
BRYAN KENNEDY and JIM RUSHING

American Honky-Tonk Bar Association - 6 - 1

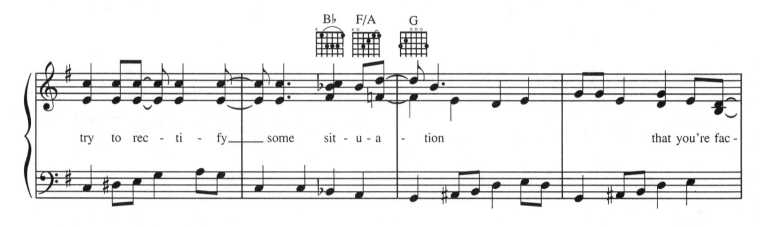

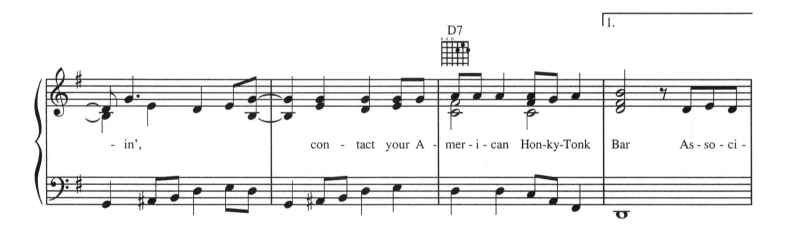

282

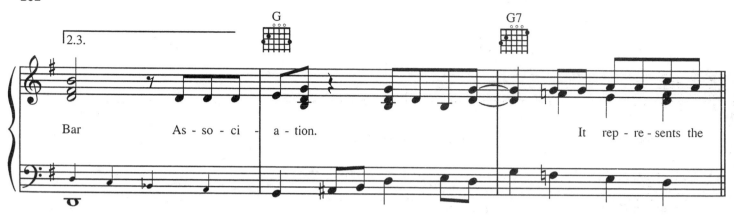

Chorus:

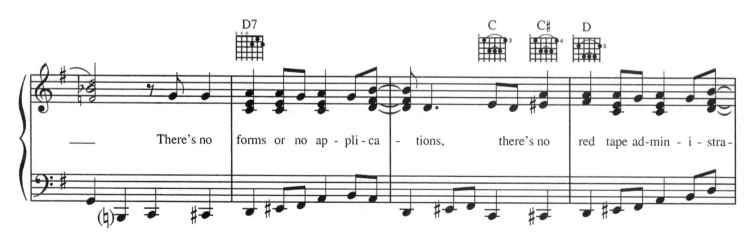

American Honky-Tonk Bar Association - 6 - 3

To Coda ⊕

- tions; it's the A - mer - i - can Hon-ky-Tonk Bar As - so - ci - a - tion.

(Instrumental solo . . .

. . . end solo)

D.S. % al Coda

3. We're

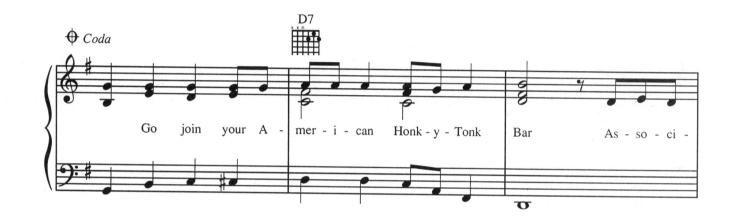

Go join your A - mer - i - can Honk - y - Tonk Bar As - so - ci -

a - tion.

Do not de - lay; con - tact to - day

your A. H. B. A.,

your A. H. B. A.

3

Verse 2:
When Uncle Sam dips in your pocket,
For most things you don't mind,
But when your dollar goes to all of those
Standing in a welfare line,
Rejoice, you have a voice,
If you're concerned about the destination
Of this great nation:
It's called the American Honky-Tonk Bar Association.
(To Chorus:)

Verse 3:
We're all one big family,
Throughout the cities and the towns.
We don't reach for handouts;
We reach for those who are down.
And every local chapter has a seven day a week
Available consultation
For your frustration.
It's called an American Honky-Tonk Bar Association.
(To Chorus:)

ANONYMOUS

Words and Music by
TONY ARATA and JON SCHWABE

Verse 1:

wrote our names__ a thou-sand times__ just to see yours____ sit-ting next to mine,__ then

sent you flow-ers, card un-signed;__ A-non-y-mous.__ In

STANDING OUTSIDE THE FIRE

Words and Music by
JENNY YATES and GARTH BROOKS

*L.H. tacet verses 1 & 2 on recording.
**Chords in parentheses are played 2nd time only.

Standing Outside the Fire - 5 - 1

Chorus:

Stand-ing__ out-side the fire.__ Stand-ing__ out-side the fire.__

__ Life is__ not tried, it__ is mere-ly__ sur-vived if__ you're

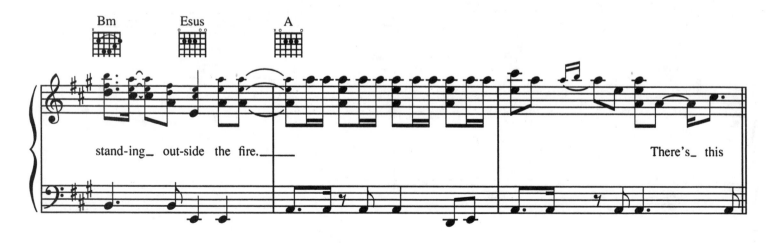

stand-ing__ out-side the fire.__ There's__ this

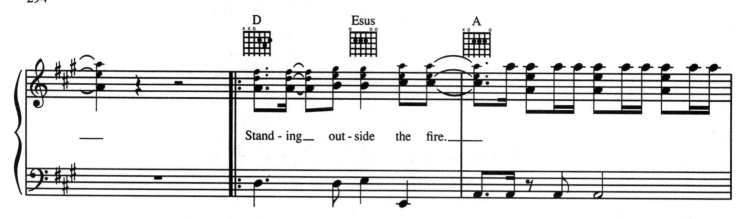

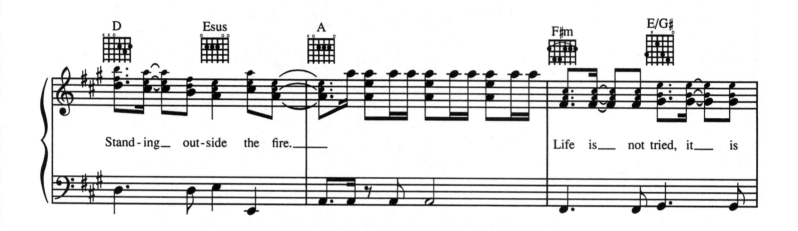

Verse 2:
We call them strong,
Those who can face this world alone,
Who seem to get by on their own,
Those who will never take the fall.
We call them weak,
Who are unable to resist
The slightest chance love might exist,
And for that forsake it all.
They're so hell bent on giving, walking a wire,
Convinced it's not living if you stand outside the fire.
(To Chorus:)

F R E S H   H O R S E S

The Beaches Of Cheyenne 296

The Change 300

Cowboys And Angels 304

The Fever 312

Ireland 307

It's Midnight Cinderella 318

The Old Stuff 326

Rollin' 333

She's Every Woman 340

That Ol' Wind 345

To Make You Feel My Love 322

THE BEACHES OF CHEYENNE

Words and Music by
BRYAN KENNEDY, DAN ROBERTS
and GARTH BROOKS

1. They packed up all___ his buck-les, and shipped his sad-dle to___ his
2.3. See additional lyrics

The Beaches of Cheyenne - 4 - 1

dad. And by the way the house____ looked, she must_ have took it

bad.____ The work-ers come_ on__ Mon - day____ to fix the

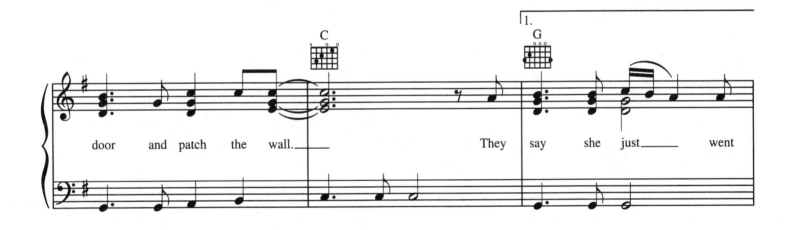

door and patch the wall.____ They say she just_____ went

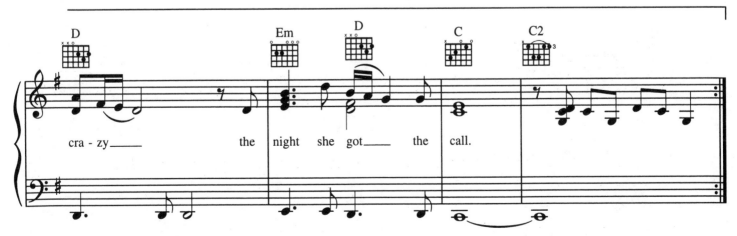

cra - zy____ the night she got___ the call.

The Beaches of Cheyenne - 4 - 2

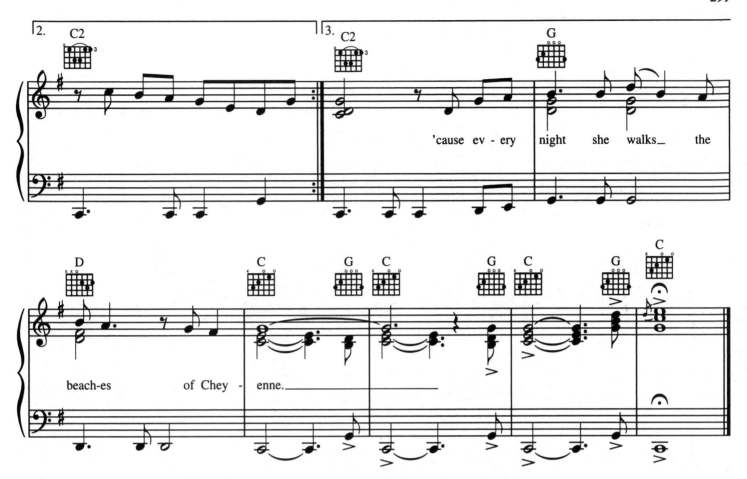

Verse 2:
Well, he was up in Wyoming,
And drew a bull no man could ride.
He promised her he'd turn out;
Well, it turned out that he lied.
And all their dreams that they'd been living
In the California sand
Died right there beside him
In Cheyenne.
(To Chorus 1:)

Verse 3:
They never found her body,
Just her diary by the bed.
It told about the fight they had,
And the words that she had said.
When he told her he was ridin',
She said, "Then I don't give a damn
If you never come back
From Cheyenne."
(To Chorus 2:)

Chorus 3:
Nobody can explain it;
Some say she's still alive.
They even claim they've seen her
On the shoreline late at night.
'Cause if you go down by the water,
You'll see her footprints in the sand,
'Cause every night, she walks the beaches
Of Cheyenne.
Yes, every night she walks the beaches
of Cheyenne.

THE CHANGE

Words and Music by
TONY ARATA and WAYNE TESTER

The Change - 4 - 1

Verse 2:
This heart still believes
That love and mercy still exist.
While all the hatreds rage, and so many say
That love is all but pointless in madness such as this;
It's like trying to stop a fire with the moisture from a kiss.
(To Chorus:)

COWBOYS AND ANGELS

Words and Music by
KENT BLAZY, KIM WILLIAMS
and GARTH BROOKS

Cowboys and Angels - 3 - 1

Verse 3:
Nothin's changed since the dawn of creation,
For you will find them together today
And only heaven above them knows why she loves him,
But he must be the reason she don't fly away.
(To Chorus:)

IRELAND

Words and Music by
STEPHANIE DAVIS, JENNY YATES
and GARTH BROOKS

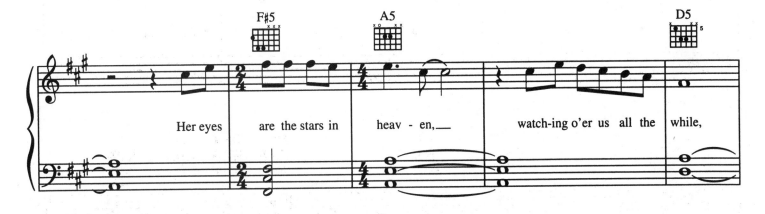

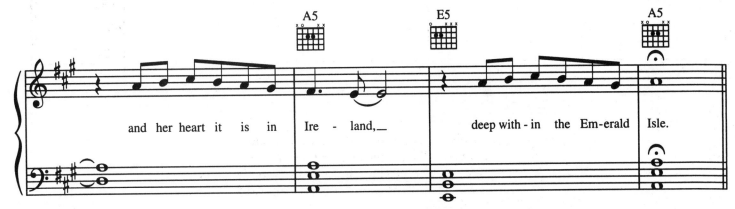

Ireland - 5 - 1

Moderately ♩=108

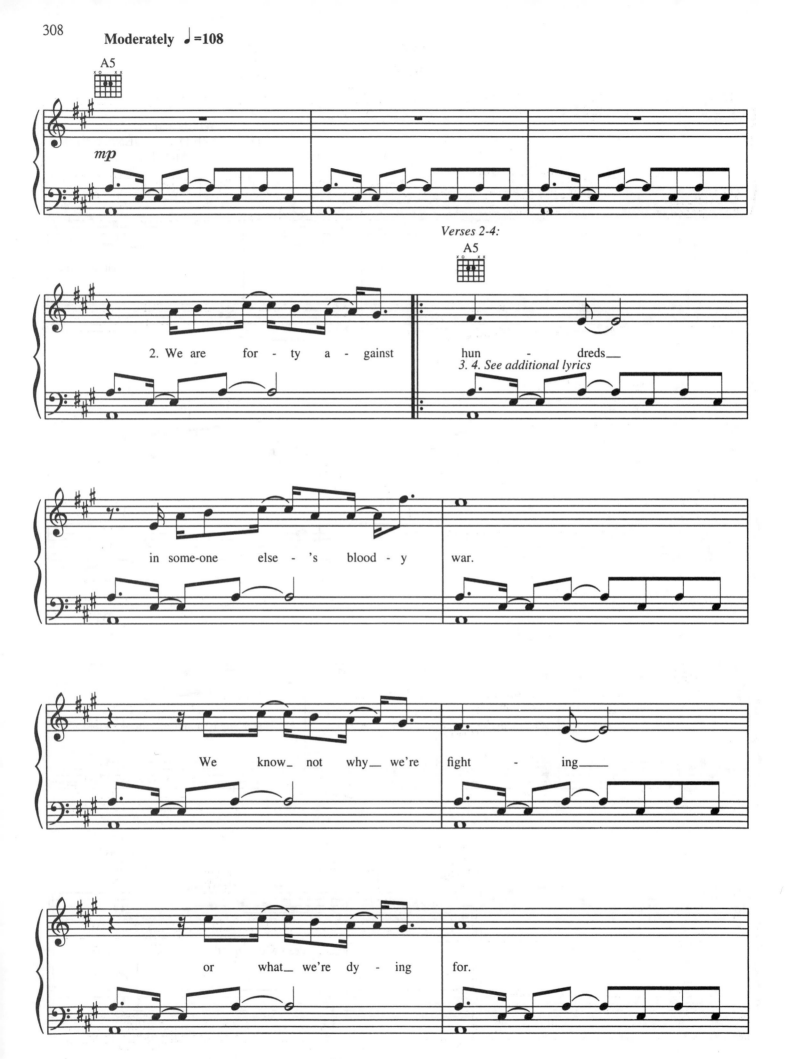

We were for - ty a - gainst hun - dreds....
(Vocal 1st time only)

Repeat ad lib. and fade

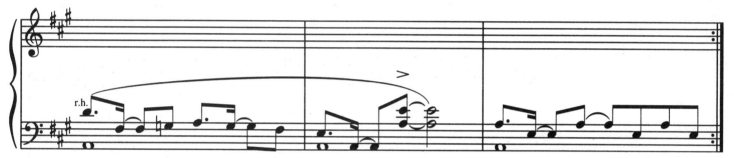

r.h.

Verse 3:
And the captain, he lay bleeding,
And I can hear him callin' me;
"These men are yours now for the leading;
Show them to their destiny."
As I look up all around me,
I see the ragged, tired and torn.
I tell them to make ready,
'Cause we're not waiting for the morn'.
(To Chorus:)

Verse 4:
Now the fog is deep and heavy
As we forge the dark and fear.
We can hear their horses breathing
As in silence we draw near.
And there are no words to be spoken,
Just a look to say "goodbye".
I draw a breath and night is broken,
As I scream our battle cry.
(To Chorus:)

THE FEVER

Words and Music by
STEVEN TYLER, JOE PERRY,
BRYAN KENNEDY and DAN ROBERTS

rid - in' like there ain't no clowns."

(Inst. solo ad lib...

3. What he
...end solo)

run-nin' from your shad-ow out of self de-fense._ But he won't run,_ and ba-by,

he can't hide;_ he thinks the odds are e-ven leav-in' one hand tied._ He

gets so tired_ of hang-in' on so tight;_ I know you think he's cra-zy, well I

think you're right._ We're all here_ 'cause he's not all there,_ that's right!

IT'S MIDNIGHT CINDERELLA

Words and Music by
KIM WILLIAMS, KENT BLAZY
and GARTH BROOKS

It's Midnight Cinderella - 4 - 1

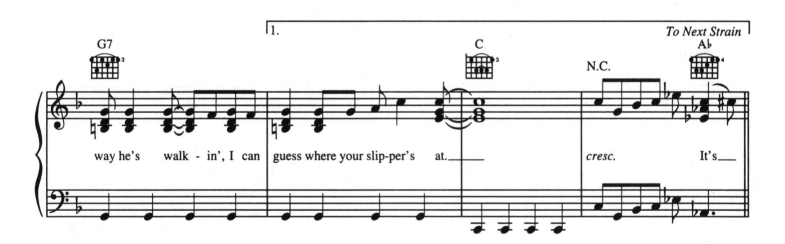

It's Midnight Cinderella - 4 - 2

Verse 2:
I'm gonna help you get over
Bein' under that spell.
You're gonna learn to love midnight
Inside this pumpkin shell.
I got a few new magic tricks
Your godmother can't do;
I'll show you what it means to
Bip, bip, bip, bip, bopity boo.
(To Chorus:)

TO MAKE YOU FEEL MY LOVE

Words and Music by
BOB DYLAN

To Make You Feel My Love - 4 - 2

324

To Make You Feel My Love - 4 - 3

To Make You Feel My Love - 4 - 4

THE OLD STUFF

Words and Music by
BRYAN KENNEDY, DAN ROBERTS
and GARTH BROOKS

...end solo)

No rules, young fools com-ing from the old school, tak-ing on the world a-lone.__

__ Next date, can't wait, tear-in' up the in-ter-state;

The Old Stuff - 7 - 6

You make me feel like the old_____ stuff_____ is new.__

Verse 2:
Oh, the stories we could tell if it weren't for the code of the road,
About the Buckboard, Bear Creek, Cowboys and the Grizzly Rose.
You know, the weather turned bad in Scottsdale;
A tornado nearly stole the show.
We just danced in the rain and listened to the thunder rolls.
(To Chorus:)

Chorus 2:
Back when the old stuff was new;
Hats off to the K. C. Opry and ellA Guru's.
It was one big party; Uncle Joe you know we owe it all to you.
Back when the old stuff was new.
(To solo:)

Chorus 3:

Repeat Chorus 1

ROLLIN'

Words and Music by
HARLEY ALLEN, LEIGH REYNOLDS
and GARTH BROOKS

Bright shuffle rock ♩=184

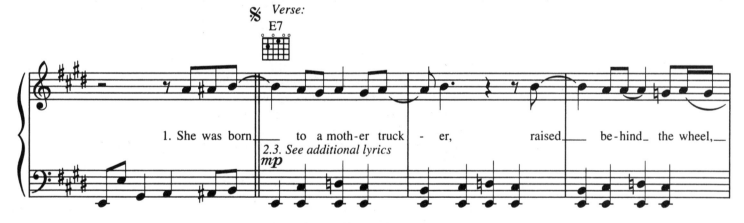

Verse:

1. She was born____ to a moth-er truck____ - er, raised____ be-hind_ the wheel,____
2.3. See additional lyrics

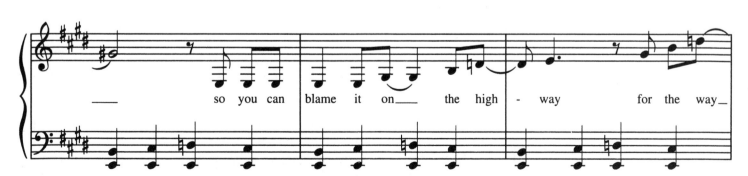

____ so you can blame it on____ the high - way for the way____

Rollin' - 7 - 1

she can't_ sit still._ She says, "Life is like a wind-shield;_ it ain't_ no rear-view mir-ror. The on-ly way to get a-where you're go-in'_____ is find that high-er gear,___ and keep it___ roll-

cresc. *mf*

To Coda ⊕

Chorus 1 & 2:

-in'.___ Life's_

f

___ gon-na run you o-ver if you don't get go-in'." She said, "I

Verse 2:
Well, I knew that I was in trouble
When she told me that talk was cheap,
Said, "If you're tired, get on the sofa,
'Cause the bed's no place to sleep."
Then she reached out and she kissed me;
Lord, it knocked me to my knees.
And I knew if I was gonna get naked,
I was gonna have to roll up my sleeves...
(To Chorus 2:)

Chorus 2:
And keep it rollin'.
Love was gonna run me over if I didn't get goin'.
She said, "I wanna feel the earth move under me,
Movin' with the motion of a melody.
Boy, I get the blues if the rhythm ain't got no soul.
You gotta keep on rollin'".
(To Bridge:)

Verse 3:
So I talked her into gettin' married,
But she wouldn't hang up her wheels.
I was afraid to take a back seat
To the way the highway feels.
But each day, she's pullin' over
More than she used to.
She knows love is like a highway;
The main thing you gotta do...
(To Chorus 3:)

SHE'S EVERY WOMAN

Words and Music by
VICTORIA SHAW and
GARTH BROOKS

She's Every Woman - 5 - 1

She's Every Woman - 5 - 2

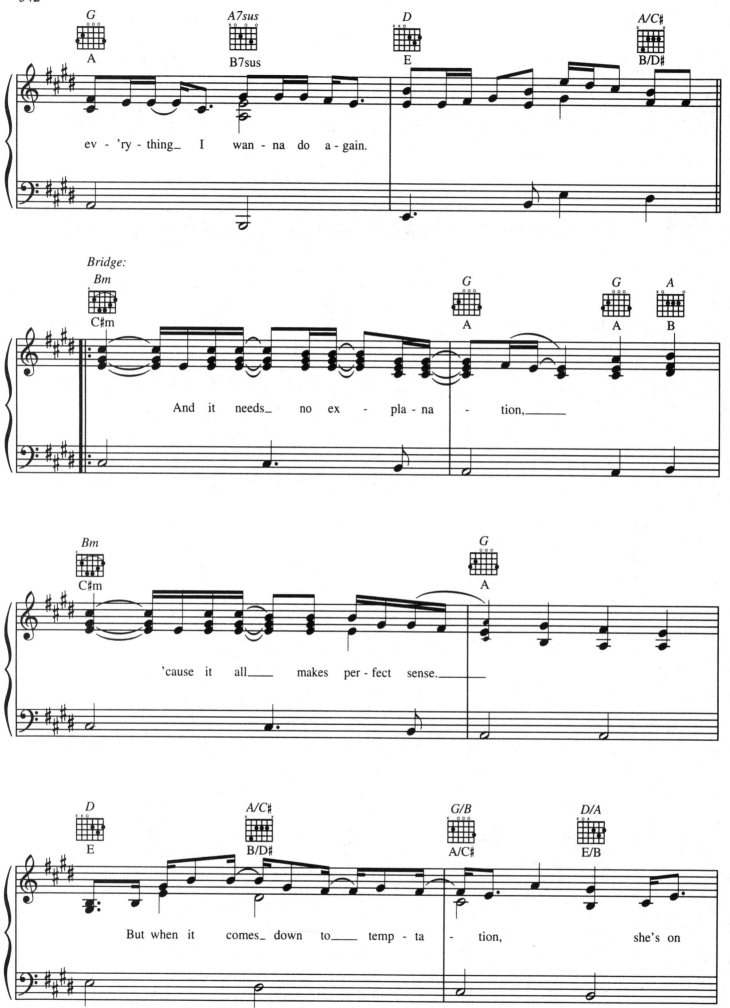

344

THAT OL' WIND

Words and Music by
LEIGH REYNOLDS and GARTH BROOKS

That Ol' Wind - 5 - 1

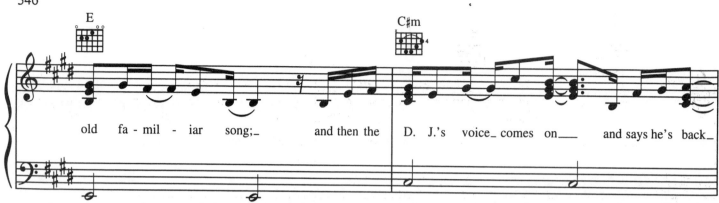

old fa - mil - iar song;___ and then the D. J.'s voice___ comes on___ and says he's back___

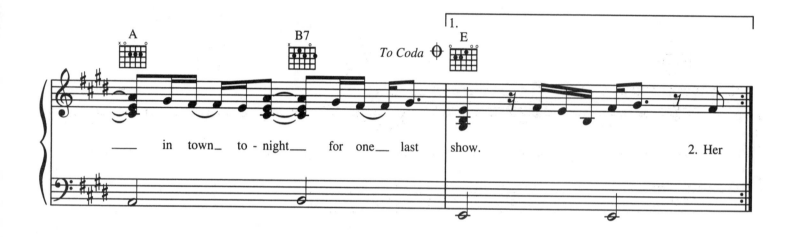

___ in town__ to - night___ for one___ last show. 2. Her

there. cresc. He asked her twice___ to come___ a - long___

2. See additional lyrics

___ they said "good - bye"___ at the break of dawn,___

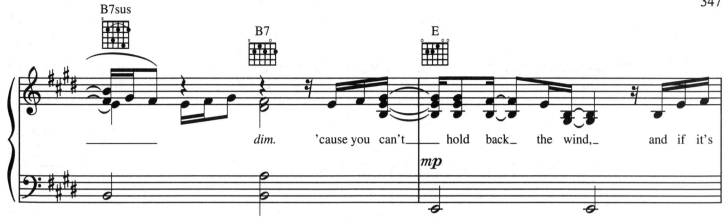

'cause you can't___ hold back___ the wind,___ and if it's

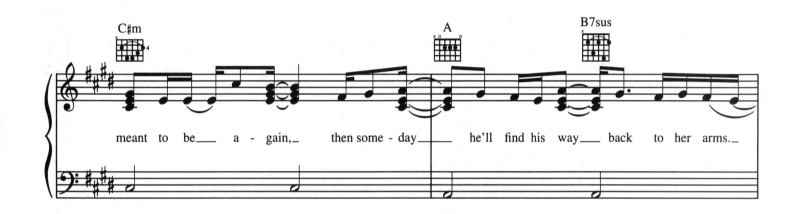

meant to be___ a - gain,___ then some - day___ he'll find his way___ back to her arms.___

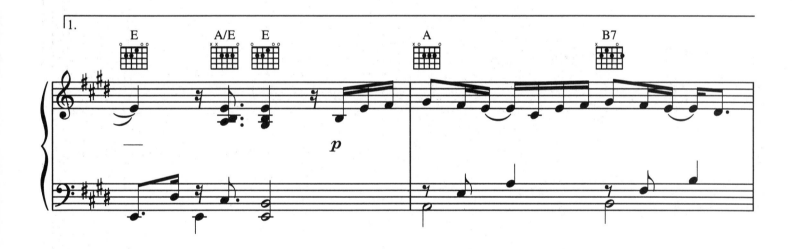

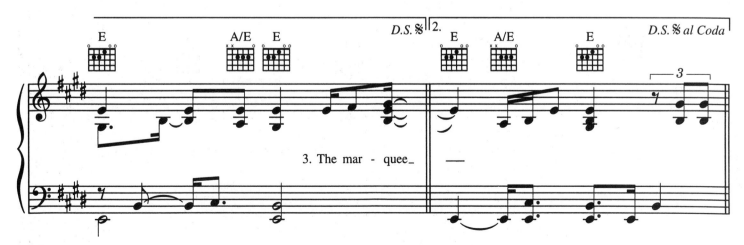

3. The mar - quee___ ___

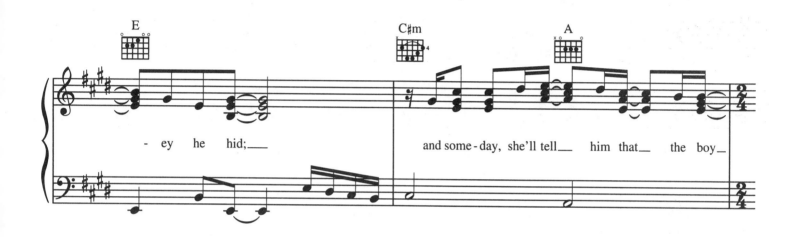

Verse 2:
Her eyes well up with tears.
God could it be? It's been ten years
Since that autumn night outside the county fair,
When two strangers shared a night,
And in the darkness, found a light
That to this day is still alive and burning there.
(To Chorus:)

Verse 3:
The marquee misspelled his name,
And not too many people came,
But that didn't matter to them.
They laughed and loved all through the night,
And as they faced the morning light,
They found themselves standing there again.

Chorus 2:
And he asked her twice to come along;
They said "goodbye" at the break of dawn.
As his bus left out, she cried,
With him standing by her side;
That ol' wind had once again found its way home.

Verse 4:
(Instrumental solo ad lib.)